Date Due

JIMMY CARTER

JIMMY CARTER

Ed Slavin

CHELSEA HOUSE PUBLISHERS
NEW YORK
PHILADELPHIA

Chelsea House Publishers
EDITOR-IN-CHIEF: Nancy Toff
EXECUTIVE EDITOR: Remmel T. Nunn
MANAGING EDITOR: Karyn Gullen Browne
COPY CHIEF: Juliann Barbato
PICTURE EDITOR: Adrian G. Allen
ART DIRECTOR: Maria Epes
MANUFACTURING MANAGER: Gerald Levine

World Leaders—Past & Present
SENIOR EDITOR: John W. Selfridge

Staff for JIMMY CARTER
ASSOCIATE EDITOR: Sean Dolan
COPY EDITOR: Terrance Dolan
DEPUTY COPY CHIEF: Ellen Scordato
EDITORIAL ASSISTANT: Heather Lewis
PICTURE RESEARCHER: Elie Porter
ASSISTANT ART DIRECTOR: Laurie Jewell
DESIGNER: David Murray
PRODUCTION COORDINATOR: Joseph Romano
COVER ILLUSTRATION: Alan J. Nahigian

First Printing

1 3 5 7 9 8 6 4 2

Library of Congress Cataloging-in-Publication Data

Slavin, Ed.
  Jimmy Carter.

  (World leaders past & present)
  Bibliography: p.
  Includes index.
  Summary: Presents the life and political career of the thirty-ninth
president of the United States.

  1. Carter, Jimmy, 1924–   —Juvenile literature. 2.
Presidents—United States—Biography—Juvenile literature.
[1. Carter, Jimmy, 1924–   . 2. Presidents] I. Title.
II. Series.
E873.S54   1988   973.926'092'4 [B] [92]   87-38196

ISBN 1-55546-828-4
     0-7910-0560-7 (pbk.)

Contents

John Adams
John Quincy Adams
Konrad Adenauer
Alexander the Great
Salvador Allende
Marc Antony
Corazon Aquino
Yasir Arafat
King Arthur
Hafez al-Assad
Kemal Atatürk
Attila
Clement Attlee
Augustus Caesar
Menachem Begin
David Ben-Gurion
Otto von Bismarck
Léon Blum
Simon Bolívar
Cesare Borgia
Willy Brandt
Leonid Brezhnev
Julius Caesar
John Calvin
Jimmy Carter
Fidel Castro
Catherine the Great
Charlemagne
Chiang Kai-Shek
Winston Churchill
Georges Clemenceau
Cleopatra
Constantine the Great
Hernán Cortés
Oliver Cromwell
Georges-Jacques
 Danton
Jefferson Davis
Moshe Dayan
Charles de Gaulle
Eamon De Valera
Eugene Debs
Deng Xiaoping
Benjamin Disraeli
Alexander Dubček
François & Jean-Claude
 Duvalier
Dwight Eisenhower
Eleanor of Aquitaine
Elizabeth I
Faisal
Ferdinand & Isabella
Francisco Franco
Benjamin Franklin

Frederick the Great
Indira Gandhi
Mohandas Gandhi
Giuseppe Garibaldi
Amin & Bashir Gemayel
Genghis Khan
William Gladstone
Mikhail Gorbachev
Ulysses S. Grant
Ernesto "Che" Guevara
Tenzin Gyatso
Alexander Hamilton
Dag Hammarskjöld
Henry VIII
Henry of Navarre
Paul von Hindenburg
Hirohito
Adolf Hitler
Ho Chi Minh
King Hussein
Ivan the Terrible
Andrew Jackson
James I
Wojciech Jaruzelski
Thomas Jefferson
Joan of Arc
Pope John XXIII
Pope John Paul II
Lyndon Johnson
Benito Juárez
John Kennedy
Robert Kennedy
Jomo Kenyatta
Ayatollah Khomeini
Nikita Khrushchev
Kim Il Sung
Martin Luther King, Jr.
Henry Kissinger
Kublai Khan
Lafayette
Robert E. Lee
Vladimir Lenin
Abraham Lincoln
David Lloyd George
Louis XIV
Martin Luther
Judas Maccabeus
James Madison
Nelson & Winnie
 Mandela
Mao Zedong
Ferdinand Marcos
George Marshall

Mary, Queen of Scots
Tomáš Masaryk
Golda Meir
Klemens von Metternich
James Monroe
Hosni Mubarak
Robert Mugabe
Benito Mussolini
Napoléon Bonaparte
Gamal Abdel Nasser
Jawaharlal Nehru
Nero
Nicholas II
Richard Nixon
Kwame Nkrumah
Daniel Ortega
Mohammed Reza Pahlavi
Thomas Paine
Charles Stewart
 Parnell
Pericles
Juan Perón
Peter the Great
Pol Pot
Muammar el-Qaddafi
Ronald Reagan
Cardinal Richelieu
Maximilien Robespierre
Eleanor Roosevelt
Franklin Roosevelt
Theodore Roosevelt
Anwar Sadat
Haile Selassie
Prince Sihanouk
Jan Smuts
Joseph Stalin
Sukarno
Sun Yat-sen
Tamerlane
Mother Teresa
Margaret Thatcher
Josip Broz Tito
Toussaint L'Ouverture
Leon Trotsky
Pierre Trudeau
Harry Truman
Queen Victoria
Lech Walesa
George Washington
Chaim Weizmann
Woodrow Wilson
Xerxes
Emiliano Zapata
Zhou Enlai

CHELSEA HOUSE PUBLISHERS

ON LEADERSHIP

Arthur M. Schlesinger, jr.

LEADERSHIP, it may be said, is really what makes the world go round. Love no doubt smooths the passage; but love is a private transaction between consenting adults. Leadership is a public transaction with history. The idea of leadership affirms the capacity of individuals to move, inspire, and mobilize masses of people so that they act together in pursuit of an end. Sometimes leadership serves good purposes, sometimes bad; but whether the end is benign or evil, great leaders are those men and women who leave their personal stamp on history.

Now, the very concept of leadership implies the proposition that individuals can make a difference. This proposition has never been universally accepted. From classical times to the present day, eminent thinkers have regarded individuals as no more than the agents and pawns of larger forces, whether the gods and goddesses of the ancient world or, in the modern era, race, class, nation, the dialectic, the will of the people, the spirit of the times, history itself. Against such forces, the individual dwindles into insignificance.

So contends the thesis of historical determinism. Tolstoy's great novel *War and Peace* offers a famous statement of the case. Why, Tolstoy asked, did millions of men in the Napoleonic Wars, denying their human feelings and their common sense, move back and forth across Europe slaughtering their fellows? "The war," Tolstoy answered, "was bound to happen simply because it was bound to happen." All prior history predetermined it. As for leaders, they, Tolstoy said, "are but the labels that serve to give a name to an end and, like labels, they have the least possible connection with the event." The greater the leader, "the more conspicuous the inevitability and the predestination of every act he commits." The leader, said Tolstoy, is "the slave of history."

Determinism takes many forms. Marxism is the determinism of class. Nazism the determinism of race. But the idea of men and women as the slaves of history runs athwart the deepest human instincts. Rigid determinism abolishes the idea of human freedom—

the assumption of free choice that underlies every move we make, every word we speak, every thought we think. It abolishes the idea of human responsibility, since it is manifestly unfair to reward or punish people for actions that are by definition beyond their control. No one can live consistently by any deterministic creed. The Marxist states prove this themselves by their extreme susceptibility to the cult of leadership.

More than that, history refutes the idea that individuals make no difference. In December 1931 a British politician crossing Park Avenue in New York City between 76th and 77th Streets around 10:30 P.M. looked in the wrong direction and was knocked down by an automobile—a moment, he later recalled, of a man aghast, a world aglare: "I do not understand why I was not broken like an eggshell or squashed like a gooseberry." Fourteen months later an American politician, sitting in an open car in Miami, Florida, was fired on by an assassin; the man beside him was hit. Those who believe that individuals make no difference to history might well ponder whether the next two decades would have been the same had Mario Constasino's car killed Winston Churchill in 1931 and Giuseppe Zangara's bullet killed Franklin Roosevelt in 1933. Suppose, in addition, that Adolf Hitler had been killed in the street fighting during the Munich *Putsch* of 1923 and that Lenin had died of typhus during World War I. What would the 20th century be like now?

For better or for worse, individuals do make a difference. "The notion that a people can run itself and its affairs anonymously," wrote the philosopher William James, "is now well known to be the silliest of absurdities. Mankind does nothing save through initiatives on the part of inventors, great or small, and imitation by the rest of us—these are the sole factors in human progress. Individuals of genius show the way, and set the patterns, which common people then adopt and follow."

Leadership, James suggests, means leadership in thought as well as in action. In the long run, leaders in thought may well make the greater difference to the world. But, as Woodrow Wilson once said, "Those only are leaders of men, in the general eye, who lead in action. . . . It is at their hands that new thought gets its translation into the crude language of deeds." Leaders in thought often invent in solitude and obscurity, leaving to later generations the tasks of imitation. Leaders in action—the leaders portrayed in this series—have to be effective in their own time.

And they cannot be effective by themselves. They must act in response to the rhythms of their age. Their genius must be adapted, in a phrase of William James's, "to the receptivities of the moment." Leaders are useless without followers. "There goes the mob," said the French politician hearing a clamor in the streets. "I am their leader. I must follow them." Great leaders turn the inchoate emotions of the mob to purposes of their own. They seize on the opportunities of their time, the hopes, fears, frustrations, crises, potentialities. They succeed when events have prepared the way for them, when the community is awaiting to be aroused, when they can provide the clarifying and organizing ideas. Leadership ignites the circuit between the individual and the mass and thereby alters history.

It may alter history for better or for worse. Leaders have been responsible for the most extravagant follies and most monstrous crimes that have beset suffering humanity. They have also been vital in such gains as humanity has made in individual freedom, religious and racial tolerance, social justice, and respect for human rights.

There is no sure way to tell in advance who is going to lead for good and who for evil. But a glance at the gallery of men and women in *World Leaders—Past and Present* suggests some useful tests.

One test is this: Do leaders lead by force or by persuasion? By command or by consent? Through most of history leadership was exercised by the divine right of authority. The duty of followers was to defer and to obey. "Theirs not to reason why / Theirs but to do and die." On occasion, as with the so-called enlightened despots of the 18th century in Europe, absolutist leadership was animated by humane purposes. More often, absolutism nourished the passion for domination, land, gold, and conquest and resulted in tyranny.

The great revolution of modern times has been the revolution of equality. The idea that all people should be equal in their legal condition has undermined the old structure of authority, hierarchy, and deference. The revolution of equality has had two contrary effects on the nature of leadership. For equality, as Alexis de Tocqueville pointed out in his great study *Democracy in America*, might mean equality in servitude as well as equality in freedom.

"I know of only two methods of establishing equality in the political world," Tocqueville wrote. "Rights must be given to every citizen, or none at all to anyone . . . save one, who is the master of all." There was no middle ground "between the sovereignty of all and the absolute power of one man." In his astonishing prediction of 20th-century totalitarian dictatorship, Tocqueville explained how the revolution of equality could lead to the *"Führerprinzip"* and more terrible absolutism than the world had ever known.

But when rights are given to every citizen and the sovereignty of all is established, the problem of leadership takes a new form, becomes more exacting than ever before. It is easy to issue commands and enforce them by the rope and the stake, the concentration camp and the *gulag.* It is much harder to use argument and achievement to overcome opposition and win consent. The Founding Fathers of the United States understood the difficulty. They believed that history had given them the opportunity to decide, as Alexander Hamilton wrote in the first Federalist Paper, whether men are indeed capable of basing government on "reflection and choice, or whether they are forever destined to depend . . . on accident and force."

Government by reflection and choice called for a new style of leadership and a new quality of followership. It required leaders to be responsive to popular concerns, and it required followers to be active and informed participants in the process. Democracy does not eliminate emotion from politics; sometimes it fosters demagoguery; but it is confident that, as the greatest of democratic leaders put it, you cannot fool all of the people all of the time. It measures leadership by results and retires those who overreach or falter or fail.

It is true that in the long run despots are measured by results too. But they can postpone the day of judgment, sometimes indefinitely, and in the meantime they can do infinite harm. It is also true that democracy is no guarantee of virtue and intelligence in government, for the voice of the people is not necessarily the voice of God. But democracy, by assuring the right of opposition, offers built-in resistance to the evils inherent in absolutism. As the theologian Reinhold Niebuhr summed it up, "Man's capacity for justice makes democracy possible, but man's inclination to injustice makes democracy necessary."

A second test for leadership is the end for which power is sought. When leaders have as their goal the supremacy of a master race or the promotion of totalitarian revolution or the acquisition and exploitation of colonies or the protection of greed and privilege or the preservation of personal power, it is likely that their leadership will do little to advance the cause of humanity. When their goal is the abolition of slavery, the liberation of women, the enlargement of opportunity for the poor and powerless, the extension of equal rights to racial minorities, the defense of the freedoms of expression and opposition, it is likely that their leadership will increase the sum of human liberty and welfare.

Leaders have done great harm to the world. They have also conferred great benefits. You will find both sorts in this series. Even "good" leaders must be regarded with a certain wariness. Leaders are not demigods; they put on their trousers one leg after another just like ordinary mortals. No leader is infallible, and every leader needs to be reminded of this at regular intervals. Irreverence irritates leaders but is their salvation. Unquestioning submission corrupts leaders and demeans followers. Making a cult of a leader is always a mistake. Fortunately hero worship generates its own antidote. "Every hero," said Emerson, "becomes a bore at last."

The signal benefit the great leaders confer is to embolden the rest of us to live according to our own best selves, to be active, insistent, and resolute in affirming our own sense of things. For great leaders attest to the reality of human freedom against the supposed inevitabilities of history. And they attest to the wisdom and power that may lie within the most unlikely of us, which is why Abraham Lincoln remains the supreme example of great leadership. A great leader, said Emerson, exhibits new possibilities to all humanity. "We feed on genius. . . . Great men exist that there may be greater men."

Great leaders, in short, justify themselves by emancipating and empowering their followers. So humanity struggles to master its destiny, remembering with Alexis de Tocqueville: "It is true that around every man a fatal circle is traced beyond which he cannot pass; but within the wide verge of that circle he is powerful and free; as it is with man, so with communities."

1

Held Captive

It was Tuesday, January 20, 1981, Jimmy Carter's last morning as president, and he was exhausted. He had been without sleep for 48 hours, most of that time spent in the Oval Office, making arrangements he hoped would bring the release of the 52 Americans held hostage by militant Iranian students in Teheran, Iran. The hostages had been in captivity since November 4, 1979, when the Iranian students, angered at Carter's decision to allow the deposed leader of their nation, Shah Mohammed Reza Pahlavi, to receive medical treatment in the United States for his liver cancer, overran the American embassy. During the 444 days that had since elapsed, Carter had tried economic sanctions, diplomatic initiatives, and the threat of military action to gain the hostages' release. He had frozen approximately $12 billion in Iranian assets in the form of gold and cash on deposit in American banks in the United States and abroad, but the Iranians had continued to insist on the return of the shah and the $3 billion he was said to have spirited out of the country with him as the price of the hostages' release.

The release of the American hostages had almost become an obsession to me.
—JIMMY CARTER

After learning that a top-secret attempt to rescue the 53 American hostages held in the U.S. embassy in Iran ended in disaster, a careworn Jimmy Carter ponders their fate in April 1980. Millions of Americans shared Carter's frustration as the 444-day hostage crisis took its toll on the nation.

Most frustrating of all Carter's efforts had been the failed April 1980 rescue attempt. The plan called for a 90-man specially trained strike team — the Delta Force — to be ferried, under cover of darkness, aboard 3 C-130 airliners to a landing site in the Iranian desert approximately 300 miles southeast of Teheran. There they would rendezvous with eight helicopters. Men, fuel, and supplies would be transferred from the planes to the helicopters, which would then fly to a hiding place in the mountains, south of Teheran. By this time it would be almost daybreak. The Delta Force would spend the daylight hours in the mountains while U.S. intelligence agents assembled the fleet of trucks they had purchased in the weeks leading up to the operation. At nightfall the trucks would be driven into the mountains and used to carry the Delta Force into Teheran. Intelligence reports had revealed the exact whereabouts of the hostages within the embassy compound and that Iranian security had grown lax. The Delta Force planned to enter the compound, overpower the guards, and release the hostages. Upon receipt of radio communications indicating that the hostages had been freed, the helicopters would pick up the Americans at prearranged landing sites near the embassy and take them to an abandoned airstrip on the outskirts of Teheran. Two giant C-141s would then fly the hostages and the Delta Force to safety in Saudi Arabia.

Carter's decision to proceed with the rescue attempt cost him the services of his secretary of state, Cyrus Vance, who believed that the mission might endanger the safety of the hostages and who thought further negotiations a more prudent course. Vance resigned on April 21, three days before the rescue was due to take place, although his leaving and the reason for it did not become public until later.

At least six helicopters were needed for the successful implementation of the mission. Eight choppers left a U.S. aircraft carrier in the Gulf of Oman at approximately 10:00 A.M., eastern standard time, on the morning of Thursday, April 24. In Iran it was about 7:30 the previous evening. Night was falling.

In Teheran, the capital of Iran, Ayatollah Ruhollah Khomeini bestows a blessing upon a throng of supporters on February 3, 1979, two days after returning from exile. Khomeini, a fundamentalist Muslim, assumed leadership of Iran following a revolution that overthrew the hated shah.

Iranian militants patrol the front gate of the American embassy where the 53 American hostages were held. The militants, who called themselves students, overran the embassy on November 4, 1979, to protest what they considered U.S. interference in Iranian affairs.

On their way to Desert One, as the first rendezvous site was known, the helicopters encountered severe dust storms. One chopper turned back and returned to the aircraft carrier; another was forced down in the desert. Its crew was picked up, but the copter itself was abandoned. The three C-130s arrived at Desert One as scheduled, but to the Americans' surprise, three motor vehicles drove by on the lonely desert road near the landing site. Two of the vehicles — a fuel truck and a pickup truck, probably engaged in smuggling gasoline — got away. The Delta Force detained the third vehicle, a bus containing 44 passengers, and herded its occupants aboard a C-130 for transport to Egypt until the operation was over.

None of these unexpected occurrences was deemed to endanger the mission. The helicopters refueled, but one had developed mechanical difficulties. That left only five helicopters, one less than the minimum needed. Ground commander Colonel Charles Beckwith recommended that the mission be aborted, as did mission commander General James Vaught, in Egypt. At 4:57 P.M., Washington time, Carter terminated the rescue mission. As the helicopters maneuvered to leave room for the C-130s to take off, one crashed into the nose of the jetliner. (Because the wash from the helicopter blades had kicked up sand at Desert One, visibility was extremely poor.) Both aircraft burst into flames. Eight Americans were killed, and three others were badly burned. The corpses of the dead Americans were left behind as the five remaining C-130s departed for Masirah, a small island off Oman.

The wreckage of one of the U.S. Delta Force helicopters involved in the ill-fated attempt to rescue the American hostages. The mission became a debacle when one of the helicopters crashed and burned in the Iranian desert. Eight U.S. marines were killed.

The American people were stunned by news of the rescue mission's failure. For months they had watched filmed reports on nightly newscasts showing crowds of Iranians in the streets of Teheran chanting "death to America." The rhetoric of the Ayatollah Khomeini, Iran's leader after the Shah, characterized the United States as the "Great Satan." Accustomed to thinking of their nation as the world's premier power, with the ability to affect events around the globe, Americans were frustrated by their government's irresoluteness regarding the hostage crisis. Such frustration revealed itself in bumper stickers reading Nuke Iran and a song entitled "Bomb Iran," set to the melody of a Beach Boys' hit of years past, "Barbara Ann." The hostage crisis and failure of the rescue mission seemed to confirm that the United States had become a second-rate power. Carter was roundly criticized. Liberals took Vance's position that the mission itself had threatened the well-being of the hostages. Conservatives questioned why a rescue action or military strike had not been authorized sooner. Questions were raised about the planning of the mission. The intelligence reports stating that the road near Desert One was rarely used were attacked. The military was criticized for failing to prepare its men and machinery for desert warfare. The entire plan was characterized as unrealistic and hastily prepared. Vance's resignation was cited as an example of the disharmony that was said to reign within the administration; Carter was portrayed as disorganized and indecisive. His approval rating in public opinion polls sank to 20 percent.

To make matters worse for Carter, 1980 was an election year. The hostage crisis cast its shadow over the entire campaign. Carter's poor showing in the polls led to a challenge from a fellow Democrat, Senator Edward Kennedy of Massachusetts, for their party's nomination. Despite his reported unpopularity, Carter vowed to "whip [Kennedy's] ass" in the primaries (statewide elections designed to determine a candidate's popularity among the members of his own party, used for the allocation of delegates to the party's nominating convention). His confidence was not misplaced. Carter did indeed win the Democratic nomination — an incumbent president had never been denied his party's nomination for reelection — but the long and bruising primary campaign left the Democrats divided as they began the fall campaign against the Republican nominee — Ronald Reagan, a former radio broadcaster, movie actor, and governor of California.

But even more damaging to Carter's chances was his failure to resolve the hostage crisis. He continued to pursue negotiations but met with only more frustration. The situation within Iran was chaotic. Representatives of the Iranian government would give their approval of conditions one day, then renege the next. No one could be certain whether the government's representatives should be listened to at all, for it was apparent that the only leader within Iran able to exercise power was the Ayatollah Khomeini. Not even the death of the shah, in July 1980, ended the stalemate.

At home, Reagan hammered away at Carter's "softness," asserting that were he to be elected he would not hesitate to use military action against terrorists. Carter had been delighted that the Republicans had chosen Reagan, who he believed "was the weakest candidate the Republicans could have chosen." In his presidential memoirs, *Keeping Faith*, Carter wrote that "it seemed inconceivable that [Reagan] would be acceptable as President when his positions were exposed clearly to the public."

A New Jersey marksman takes aim at a target bearing the image of Ayatollah Khomeini at a "turkey shoot" sponsored by a local fire department. The hostage crisis gave rise to vehement anti-Iranian sentiment across the United States and Khomeini became something of a bogeyman to the American public.

Carter badly underestimated Reagan's public appeal. More than the hostage crisis stood between Carter and reelection: The economy had suffered from high inflation, unemployment, and recession during his presidency, and Carter's remedies — limits on government expenditures and a refusal to cut taxes — were unpopular, particularly when the economy did not respond. His efforts to establish a comprehensive energy program, emphasizing conservation of energy and domestic production of oil, seemed to imply to some Americans that the nation was being figuratively held hostage by the oil-producing Arab nations of OPEC (the Organization of Petroleum Exporting Countries), a cartel that had the power to drive gasoline prices skyward. The Soviet Union had invaded Afghanistan in December 1979. Carter responded by forbidding American athletes to participate in the 1980 Summer Olympic Games, held in the Soviet capital city of Moscow. Many saw the Olympic boycott as little more than a futile gesture, underscoring America's dwindling global influence. Farmers were more upset by Carter's embargo (a legal prohibition on commerce) on grain sales to the Soviet Union.

Islamic Afghan resistance fighters travel on horseback in the rugged Doab Valley region of Afghanistan, in January 1980. The rebels were on their way to Herat, where they would raid Soviet-held positions. The Soviet Union invaded Afghanistan in December 1979, late in the third year of Carter's term as president.

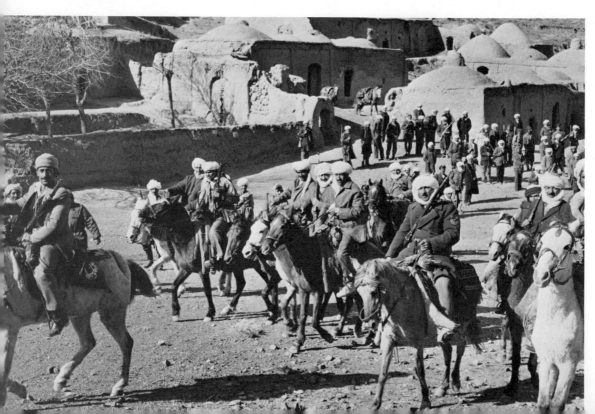

Reagan seemed to promise better. To a nation weary of being told to economize he offered a tax cut, at the same time assuring those worried by the United States's diminishing power that he would increase defense spending. His Hollywood background enabled Reagan to excel on television, whereas, by contrast, Carter appeared formal and stiff. Voters responded to Reagan's genial assertion that he would get America moving again.

Election day fell on November 4, the first anniversary of the seizure of the embassy in Teheran. More than a year before the election, in July 1979, Carter had given a nationally televised speech in which he decried the "malaise" in which the country found itself. Americans, he said, have "got to stop crying and start sweating, stop talking and start walking, stop cursing and start praying." Voters agreed that the nation was in a malaise, but they preferred to blame their leaders rather than themselves for the predicament. The election was a landslide, one of the most one-sided in American history. Reagan won 51 percent of the popular vote to Carter's 41 percent. (A third-party candidate, John An-

In March 1980, President Carter informs a gathering of American athletes and coaches that the official U.S. response to the Soviet invasion of Afghanistan will be a boycott of the 1980 Summer Olympic Games in Moscow. Carter's decision to boycott the games was an unpopular one; Olympic hopefuls were disappointed and the American public saw the boycott as a weak response to communist expansionism.

derson, took seven percent.) The electoral vote breakdown was even more lopsided. Two hundred and seventy electoral votes constituted a majority; Reagan polled 489, Carter only 49. Much had been made of Carter's being the first president from the Deep South in nearly 130 years, but in his bid for reelection Carter won only two of the southern states, Georgia and Maryland.

In the two and a half months between the election and Reagan's inauguration, Carter continued his efforts to free the hostages. He was aided now by diplomats from Algeria (Algeria had volunteered to act as an intermediary in the crisis). Carter assented to the basic Iranian demands — release of the frozen Iranian assets and a pledge that the United States would not intervene in Iranian affairs — but balked at further conditions, such as turning over $25 billion to Algeria as an indemnity (security) against future claims by Iran. Iraq's September invasion of Iran had made the situation even more tumultuous, greatly complicating negotiations. Iranian government ministers made various pledges to the Algerians, but only the enigmatic Khomeini had the power to approve the hostages' release. Several times a deal appeared to have been made, only to fall apart at the last moment.

Carter persisted, and by his final weekend in office it appeared a bargain had been struck. The United States agreed to free the frozen Iranian assets and pledged not to interfere in Iranian affairs in exchange for the return of the hostages. The deal required extremely complex financial transactions. Two-thirds of the Iranian funds would be transferred out of American control. The remaining funds would be unfrozen but would remain in American banks, where they would be subject to claims from both sides. Those claims would be settled by international arbitration. Making sure that every detail of the transaction was in order, Carter spent the last 48 hours of his term in the White House, speaking by phone with diplomats in Algiers, the capital of Algeria, and in London, where the majority of the Iranian gold was to be placed in an escrow account in the Bank of England.

It is impossible for me to put into words how much the hostages had come to mean to me, or how moved I was . . . to know they were coming home.
—JIMMY CARTER

At 8:18 on the morning of the 20th, Carter received notification that the funds had been transferred to the escrow account. Under the terms of the agreement, Iran was now to "bring about the safe departure of the 52 U.S. nationals detained in Iran." Ten minutes later Carter learned that the jets that would carry the hostages from Iran were ready on the runway at Teheran's airport. Inexplicably, there was further delay. At 9:45 Deputy Secretary of State Warren Christopher, who had conducted many of the negotiations, told Carter from Algiers that the Iranians had promised the planes would depart by noon, Washington time. An hour later, Carter's wife, Rosalynn, entered the Oval Office to inform him that the Reagans would be arriving at the White House in 15 minutes and that he should change into his formal wear for the inaugural ceremonies. Carter departed for the Capitol and the inauguration still not knowing whether the hostages had actually been released. Shortly before 1:00 a Secret Service agent notified him that the planes had taken off with the hostages on board and were making their way to an American military hospital in West Germany, where the hostages would be examined, reunited with their families, and allowed to rest before continuing homeward. The news, Carter wrote, made his day of departure from office "even happier than that day exactly four years earlier," when President Gerald Ford had greeted him on the way to his own inauguration.

Chief Justice Warren Burger (foreground, right) administers the oath of office to newly elected president Ronald Reagan in Washington, D.C., on January 20, 1981. Reagan's wife, Nancy, looks on proudly. Behind the chief justice stand Senator Mark Hatfield and Jimmy Carter.

2

Marching Through Georgia

James Earl Carter, Jr., was born on October 1, 1924, in the small town — population 550 — of Plains, Georgia. Three years later the Carters moved to a farm in the hamlet of Archery, two miles away. Both Plains and Archery are located in rural Sumter County, in the southwestern part of the state. The Carters were 1 of 2 white families in Archery; there were perhaps 20 black families in the hamlet. Most of the blacks were sharecroppers on Carter's father's land. As an adult, Carter remembered that his childhood "was spent in a fairly isolated way, out in the woods and in the streams and swamps and fields. . . . My whole environment was completely rural." To get to Plains from Archery young Jimmy had to walk two miles along the railroad tracks.

In a 1976 interview with *Washington Post* columnist William Greider, Carter said that his "favorite book of all time" was *Let Us Now Praise Famous Men*, a poetic evocation by James Agee, with photographs by Walker Evans, of the bleak

> *I come from a good family and I want you all to be part of my family.*
> —JIMMY CARTER

Newlyweds Jimmy and Rosalynn Carter at the Plains Methodist Church in Plains, Georgia, on their wedding day, July 7, 1946. The groom, in formal naval dress, had recently graduated from the U.S. Naval Academy at Annapolis, Maryland.

The newly elected 39th president of the United States is welcomed home with a hug from his mother, Lillian Carter. The president inherited many valuable qualities from Mrs. Carter, who worked long days as a nurse and devoted much of her spare time to providing health care to local sharecroppers.

existence of three families of white Alabama tenant farmers during the Great Depression. Agee's book, Carter said, was an "analysis of the way I lived. That was the way I grew up." Yet Carter's childhood was somewhat less harsh than the lives of the Gudgers, the Richetts, and the Woods, the families depicted by Agee and Evans.

There had been Carters living in and around Plains for more than 100 years before Jimmy's birth. By completing the tenth grade of the Riverside Academy in Gainesville, Jimmy's father, James Earl, Sr., received, in his son's words, the "most advanced education of any Carter man since our family moved to Georgia." After service in the army during World War I, Earl, as he preferred to be called, returned to Plains and began dabbling in farming and land speculation. His industriousness caught the eye of Dr. Samuel Wise, one of three brothers who ran the private hospital in Plains. Wise told a young nurse on his staff, Bessie Lillian Gordy, that she ought to drop her current boyfriend in favor of Earl Carter: "He's a boy that has more ambition than anybody in this town, and he's going to be worth a lot someday."

Lillian Gordy was notoriously independent, so it is uncertain how much heed she gave to Wise's advice, but she was soon introduced to Earl at a local dance. Two years later, in 1923, Lillian and Earl were married. They did not honeymoon; Earl had planted potatoes to finance their trip, but the crop failed. Nevertheless, the business savvy that led Earl's brother, William Alton Carter, to characterize him as a "wizard" was soon in evidence. His reputation in Plains was sufficent for him to qualify for a loan, which he used to purchase a farm in Archery. The farm prospered, and Earl bought another and then a third. In a short time his holdings totaled 4,000 acres, worked by 200 black sharecroppers. He branched out into commodities brokering, particularly in peanut futures, and bought an office in Plains, which was soon doubling as a storeroom for his seed and fertilizer business. Carter's Warehouse, as the Plains establishment was soon known, also housed Earl's insurance business. Next door to the family's Archery home Earl opened a grocery and general store. It catered primarily to the black sharecroppers who lived on and worked his land. Earl Carter also served as one of Sumter County's more reliable financial institutions. His brother Alton estimated that virtually every one of the 600 white farmers in the region borrowed money or received credit from Earl Carter at one time or another. Finally, Earl Carter was active in local and state politics. He was a longtime member of the county board of education and was elected to the state legislature in 1952.

Jimmy Carter's father was short and stout, about 5 feet 8 inches tall and nearsighted, with thinning sandy hair. In his autobiography, *Why Not the Best?*, Carter remembered his father as an imposing physical presence, "a stern disciplinarian [who] punished me severely when I misbehaved. From the time I was four years old until I was fifteen years old, he whipped me six times, and I've never forgotten any of those impressive experiences." Earl Carter was an extremely hard worker, whose various responsibilities kept him busy from before dawn until well after nightfall. He expected a great deal

A 13-year-old Jimmy Carter strikes a Tom Sawyer—like pose in this 1938 snapshot taken near his home in Plains. As a boy, Carter worked hard on his father's farm, but he could always find time to indulge in his favorite pastime, reading.

from his firstborn child. As a very young boy, Jimmy worked carrying buckets of water from a creek to his father's field hands. When he got a little older, Jimmy joined the sharecroppers in the fields during planting and harvesting season. His day lasted from 4:00 A.M. until dark, with breaks for breakfast and dinner and to "let the mules rest." Young Jimmy received a quarter a day for his labors; the sharecroppers got $1.25.

There was a more easygoing side to Earl Carter as well. The third Carter child, Ruth, remembers growing up in an "overly protective environment" where she "never had to wash a dish or launder underwear." Jimmy's sister Gloria, who was five years younger than he, recalled that the family "had a bicycle, a trapeze under the tree, a tennis court. We had a horse to ride and a pond to fish in. He [Earl] enjoyed these as much as we did." According to Gloria, her father enjoyed music and was a good dancer, a recollection her mother confirms. According to Lillian, she and her husband also enjoyed a regular bourbon nightcap, although they were careful to keep such indulgences a secret from their children.

Although Carter concedes that his father could be "an exuberant man," it was Earl's more austere side that exerted the greatest influence on his firstborn. Gloria recalled in a February 1977 interview, "Daddy always wanted Jimmy to go straight to the top. No matter how well Jimmy did, Daddy always said he could do better." In addition to his work on the farm, Jimmy was expected to excel academically. Any grade lower than an A was unacceptable. The elder Carter enjoyed playing cards, tennis, and baseball and passed on those enthusiasms — as well as a fierce desire to win — to Jimmy. Gloria remembered that "even when we were little, we had to play against him [Earl] to win."

Lillian Carter's influence was quite different. Carter wrote of her: "My mother is a registered nurse, and during my formative years she worked constantly, primarily on private duty either at the nearby hospital or in patients' homes. She typically worked on nursing duty twelve hours per day, or twenty hours per day for which she was paid a magnificent six dollars, and during her off-duty hours she had to perform the normal functions of a mother and a housekeeper. She served as a community doctor for our neighbors and for us, and was extremely compassionate towards all those who were afflicted with any sort of illness." Lillian worked out an arrangement with Dr. Wise whereby he would provide free medical care for the sharecroppers, who could

My daddy worked hard and was a meticulous planner like me, but he was an exuberant man.
—JIMMY CARTER

not afford doctors' fees, if she would donate her nursing services. Sometimes Lillian received payments of chickens, a ham, eggs, fresh clean fish, or "perhaps a possum or two for her work." Annie Mae Jones, a black neighbor who helped raise the Carter children, confirms Lillian Carter's dedication: "Miss Lillian, she nursed day and night. She was just like a doctor. If anyone got sick on the place, she'd be right there. . . . She'd leave in the evening and she wouldn't be back until the next morning."

Jimmy Carter's recollections aside, it is clear that his mother's devotion to nursing kept her from many of the domestic tasks regarded as "woman's work" in the rural South. As a child, Carter was cared for by a succession of black nannies, among them Annie Mae Jones, who recalled that when Lillian Carter was called away, "I knew what to do. And I'd say, well, I'll stay with the children — cook, feed them. If they had to go to school, I'd get them off. I was right there every day." Lillian Carter hated to cook; when Earl Carter returned from the fields or his warehouse for his three daily meals, it was often Annie Mae Jones or one of her successors who prepared them. Lillian's chief role at home seems to have been as an intermediary between Earl and the children. She felt that her husband could sometimes be too strict, and she particularly disliked seeing the children physically punished.

Lillian Carter's independence set her apart from most Sumter County women. She recalls having no close friends. Her greatest passion was for literature, and she delighted in indulging in what she called "orgies of reading." Books were her gift of choice to her children on birthdays or Christmas, and she instilled a similar love of reading in her son Jimmy. Lillian's favorite writer was the great 19th-century Russian novelist Fyodor Dostoevsky; Jimmy's favorite novel is *War and Peace*, by Dostoevsky's countryman and contemporary Leo Tolstoy, which he read for the first time when he was 12 years old. Mother and son also admired the novels and short stories of the Amercan southern writer William Faulkner.

> *My mother is a registered nurse, and during my formative years she worked constantly.*
> —JIMMY CARTER

One other element in Lillian Carter's character differentiated her from the typical residents of Sumter County. In a time and place when segregation was both a rigidly defined social code and the law of the land, Lillian Carter was something of a beacon of racial tolerance. Not only did she minister to the health of black sharecroppers, but she also attended the funeral when one of them died. On more than one occasion she was bold enough to receive a black caller, Alvan Johnson, son of the bishop of the African Methodist Episcopal Church, at the front door of the Carter home and then entertain him in the living room. Jimmy's father was more traditional: As southern mores mandated, his black callers came to the back door, which is where whatever business they had with "Mr. Earl" was conducted, and even so prominent a fixture in the black community as Bishop Johnson sent his driver to the back door when he wished to speak with Mr. Earl. The two men would then talk outside in the Carters' yard.

Nazi dictator Adolf Hitler greets spectators at the 1936 Olympic Games in the German city of Berlin. Hitler intended to use the Berlin games as a showcase for the talents of German athletes, but his hopes faded as he watched the triumphant performance of black American track-and-field superstar Jesse Owens, who won four gold medals.

Earl Carter was a supporter of Eugene Talmadge, Georgia's governor from 1933 to 1937 and 1941 to 1943. Talmadge was a classic southern demagogue, who, in the words of historian George Tindall, preached the virtues of "work, thrift, individualism, and piety" to poor white Georgians while preying on their fears of blacks. A typical Talmadge campaign address was given from a tree stump in a small Georgia town, where Old Gene, wearing his trademark horn-rimmed glasses and red suspenders, warned his listeners about how "evil nigger folk is trying to take over and kill all the white people."

In his autobiography Carter recounted another telling incident indicative of his father's racial attitudes. In 1938, heavyweight boxing champion Joe Louis, a black man, fought Max Schmeling, a German. Black Americans regarded Louis as a symbol of racial pride and achievement, whereas Schmeling was seen as embodying the noxious racial doctrines espoused by Germany's Nazi dictator, Adolf Hitler, who had already embarked on his campaign of European conquest. Two years earlier, at the Olympic Games held in the German capital of Berlin, Hitler had refused to acknowledge Jesse Owens, the black American track and field star who had won four gold medals. That same year Schmeling had defeated Louis in a nontitle bout. It was the only loss Louis had suffered.

The night of the fight a crowd of about 40 or 50 black sharecroppers gathered at the Carter home. Mr. Earl owned the only radio for miles around; the blacks had come to ask if they could listen to the broadcast of the fight. The radio was propped in an open window, and the blacks gathered under a large mulberry tree in the yard outside. Louis knocked Schmeling out within two minutes of the first round. Carter wrote that his father "was deeply disappointed in the outcome. There was no sound from anyone in the yard, except a polite 'Thank you, Mr. Earl' offered to my father." The Carters' guests left quietly. When they arrived at one of their own cabins, 100 yards away across the railroad tracks, "pandemonium broke loose inside the house, as our black neighbors shouted and yelled in celebration of the Louis victory."

The southern racial caste system was in ways schizophrenic. Few whites challenged the southern "way of life," yet Jimmy Carter's childhood playmates were mostly black children. His best friend until the time he was 14 was A. B. Davis, a black child. Yet it is doubtful whether the young Jimmy Carter questioned his privileged role as the eldest son of the most important white landowner in the area. In *Why Not the Best?* he admits that "as a child, I rode a bus to school each day with the other white students, while the black children walked, and never gave a thought to the lack of equality inherent in the separateness." His memoirs also tell the story of how as a nine-year-old boy he used the money from the sale of boiled peanuts to purchase five bales of cotton, which he stored until the price of cotton rose. The profit he then made on the sale of the cotton was used to purchase five clapboard sharecroppers' shacks, for which he collected

New York boxing fans in Harlem celebrate the victory of heavyweight champion Joe Louis over Max Schmeling on June 22, 1938. Schmeling, the pride of Nazi Germany, was knocked out by "the Brown Bomber" in the first round. Like many Germans and white Americans, Earl Carter, Jimmy's father, was stunned by Schmeling's defeat at the hands of a black man.

Jimmy Carter presented this photograph of himself to his bride-to-be, Rosalynn Smith, while on leave from the U.S. Naval Academy at Annapolis. The couple married as soon as Jimmy graduated from the academy.

$16.50 in monthly rent for the next 15 years. After the Civil War, sharecropping had replaced slavery as the means by which white landowners held blacks in economic bondage; Carter's youthful business acumen suggests that he had been groomed to inherit his rightful place near the top of the southern economic structure.

Jimmy learned the necessity for discipline and hard work at a young age. He excelled at school in Plains, where his English teacher, Julia Coleman, encouraged his love of reading. Free time was spent on the myriad chores Earl Carter had him perform, the most odious, from young Jimmy's point of view, being cotton mopping — daubing cotton plants with a rag mop soaked in a homemade sticky pesticide composed of arsenic, molasses, and water designed to keep off boll weevils (a boll weevil is a type of insect that poses a serious threat to cotton crops). As Jimmy applied the remedy to acres of cotton plants, his trousers, legs, and bare feet would become "saturated with the syrupy mess," becoming so soaked in the stuff that he had to stand his pants in a corner at day's end "because the legs wouldn't bend."

By all accounts Jimmy was an extremely well disciplined and obedient child, although both his sisters and his mother recall that he liked nothing better than teasing his sisters and playing practical jokes on them. Although in later years Carter remembered his father being "much stricter on me than many other fathers were on their children," he recalled his childhood as a generally pleasant time. "The early years of my life on the farm were full and enjoyable, isolated but not lonely," he wrote later. "We always had enough to eat, no economic hardship, but no money to waste. We felt close to nature, close to the members of our family and close to God." The Carters were Baptists. They regularly attended the Sunday services at the Plains Baptist Church, and Lillian impressed upon Jimmy her belief in the efficacy of private prayer. Jimmy was baptized at age 11; the following year he began borrowing his mother's black Plymouth on Sunday mornings to pick up classmates who had no other way to get to church.

From the age of four or five Carter was determined to attend the U.S. Naval Academy at Annapolis, even though he "did not have a clear concept even of what Annapolis was." Indeed, until he got to Annapolis, Carter had never even seen the ocean. His fascination seems to have been inspired by the example of his uncle Thomas Gordy, a navy enlisted man. Jimmy sent for the admissions catalog, memorized its requirements, and tailored his studies to fit them. More worrisome were the academy's physical requirements. He worried that his overbite might disqualify him, spent hours rolling Coca Cola bottles on the soles of his feet to guard against flat feet,

James Earl . . . set seemingly impossible standards of performance for his children, especially Jimmy.
—BRUCE MAZLISH
Carter biographer

Lieutenant Jimmy Carter monitors operations on the bridge of the navy submarine USS *K-1* in 1952. Carter's fellow crewmen remember him as an officer who inspired confidence and loyalty through a reserved and understated style of leadership.

and stuffed himself with food for fear that he would be ineligible for appointment because of his small size (only 5 feet 3 inches and 121 pounds at the time of his high school graduation). Earl Carter did his part by cultivating his local congressman, Stephen Pace. (Admission to the service academies is by congressional appointment. There is no tuition or other charges; in exchange for their education cadets pledge to serve for a certain number of years as an officer in their particular branch of the military.)

Carter finished the 11th and final grade in the Plains school in 1941. Representative Pace had not yet been able to obtain an appointment for him, so Carter began college at Georgia Southwestern College in nearby Americus. He attended classes there for a year. When his appointment came through, to begin in the spring of 1943, Carter enrolled at the Georgia Institute of Technology, in Atlanta, to take preparatory classes for Annapolis.

His first year at Annapolis was not easy. Carter proved to be a favorite target of the upperclassmen's hazing rituals, which most often took the form of spankings with wooden breadboards, long-handled serving spoons, and broomsticks. Carter's toothy grin first drew the upperclassmen's attention; he was singled out afterward for such offenses as repeatedly defying commands to sing "Marching Through Georgia," a ditty commemorating Union general William Tecumseh Sherman's ruinous trek from Atlanta to the sea during the Civil War. He accepted the abuse stoically, believing that "there was no way to escape" because if a plebe (first-year student) "showed any weakness, he was assaulted from all sides with punishment and harassment and forced out of the academy."

Carter came to Annapolis at the height of World War II. Although his class was on an accelerated program designed to enable it to graduate in three years rather than four, the war would be over before Carter saw active duty. He got a taste of combat during exercises in the summer of 1944, when he helped man a 40-millimeter antiaircraft gun battery and his ship had a brief encounter with a German submarine. The young man who had decided on a naval career without ever having glimpsed the ocean also discovered that he easily became seasick.

At Annapolis, Carter excelled at his studies. He graduated in June 1946 ranked 59th out of a class of 820. Like most of the people Carter would encounter in the years ahead, his classmates remembered him as intelligent, driven, of high moral character, and a trifle aloof. Few felt that they knew him well. One remembered that "Carter was very well liked by his company. But he was a loner. He did not make close intimate friendships. He went out of his way to be perhaps more friendly to more people, but he didn't need other people's close bond of friendship to support his own ego or personality —he had a very strong character."

> *[Annapolis] was sometimes a brutal form of training and testing.*
> —JIMMY CARTER

Navy rear admiral Hyman Rickover is saluted by Commander William Anderson and other officers as he boards the nuclear submarine *Nautilus* in 1958. Rickover's perfectionism and detail-oriented style of command had a lasting influence on Carter, who served under him in 1952.

One person who got to know him well was Rosalynn Smith, the best friend of his sister Ruth. Carter had known Rosalynn for years, but when he returned to Plains during a break in the school year in the summer of 1945 something about her piqued his interest. He asked Rosalynn, who was almost three years his junior, to a movie. When he returned home that night he told his mother he had just been out with the girl he was going to marry. They waited until after his graduation; the wedding took place on July 7, 1946, at the Plains Methodist Church.

The peacetime navy offered little challenge or opportunity for one as ambitious as Carter. The young married couple moved to Norfolk, Virginia, where Carter served as the electronics and photography officer aboard the U.S.S. *Wyoming* and *Missouri*. After two years of exercises and drills in the Chesapeake Bay, a frustrated Carter applied for a Rhodes scholarship, which would have enabled him to study at Oxford University in England. He was a finalist, but the screening board selected another applicant. Carter counts the failure as one of the two major setbacks of his life.

Carter rebounded quickly from his disappointment. The happiness of his marriage helped a great deal. The Carters' first son, John William, had been born in Portsmouth, Virginia, in July 1947. Despite frequent separations while Carter was aboard ship, the couple grew to be extremely close. Rosalynn has said that their early married life was particularly happy and has remembered with special fondness listening to classical music and reading Shakespeare with her husband. Carter has repeatedly characterized his wife as his "closest friend."

Shortly after his rejection by the Rhodes scholarship committee, Carter was admitted to the navy's elite submarine school at New London, Connecticut. After six months of training, he was transferred to Hawaii and given his first submarine assignment. He loved the four-month submarine cruises, although seasickness continued to plague him. His fellow officers liked and respected him, but, as always, his hard work and ambition set him apart. Shipmates recalled that he would usually work or read while they were playing poker or conversing. Although his air of reserve allowed few to get close to him, he developed a low-key leadership style that won the loyalty of those under him. His subordinates recalled that Carter was an officer who stuck up for his men.

In 1952 Carter obtained a coveted spot helping to develop one of the navy's prototype nuclear-powered submarines. His commanding officer on the project was the "father of the nuclear navy," Admiral Hyman Rickover. During his interview with Rickover for the position, Carter admitted that he had not always done his best while at the Naval Academy. Rickover's response — "Why not?" — later provided Carter with the title for his autobiography. Carter served under the extremely demanding Rickover for 11 months. Although Rickover claimed later to have only vague recollections of Carter at that time, Carter says that the admiral had a "profound effect" on his life, "perhaps more than anyone except my own parents." Rickover's style of personally overseeing every detail of his command was one Carter would later try to bring to government.

> *[Rickover] expected the maximum from us, but . . . we finally realized that no matter how hard we worked . . . he always did more himself.*
> —JIMMY CARTER

JIMMY CARTER

FOR STATE SENATOR

3

Keeping the Faith

In 1952, the same year he was elected to the Georgia state senate, Earl Carter was diagnosed as suffering from cancer. He died the following year. Over Rosalynn's strong objections, Carter resigned his commission and returned to Plains. His visits to his hometown during his navy years had been marred by frequent, often bitter quarrels with his father over racial issues. Carter's experience outside the South had led him to question racial segregation; his father, he believed, was narrow-minded if not a bigot. Earl Carter's illness caused his son to see him in a different way. Jimmy Carter remembered that in the month before Earl died more than 1,000 of his neighbors, many of them black, came to the Carter house "to bring Daddy a quail they had cooked, or a fresh loaf of bread, or some fresh-picked flowers. . . . They'd say 'I hope you give this to Mr. Earl, tell him I thank him for what he did for me.' "

He [Carter] had to come back. Everything we had was on the line.
—LILLIAN CARTER
Jimmy Carter's mother

A 1962 campaign poster urges Georgians to vote for political newcomer Jimmy Carter for the state senate. Carter lost the election to Homer Moore but succeeded in having the results invalidated by proving that the corrupt Moore had rigged the ballot. Carter won the write-in election that followed by more than 700 votes.

Attorneys George E. C. Hayes, Thurgood Marshall, and James Nabrit, Jr., (left to right) successfully argued the landmark 1954 case *Brown v. Board of Education of Topeka*, Kansas, in which the Supreme Court ruled that segregation in public schools is illegal. When Carter joined the Plains school board in 1956, the community had yet to desegregate its schools.

Because Earl Carter liked to keep his charitable acts a secret, Carter at the time did not know about his father's good deeds. That revelation came with Earl's death. As Carter and his sister Ruth informed the people around Plains that Mr. Earl had passed away, they learned that he had given many of the families money or paid tuition or medical expenses for them. On one occasion he had contributed to a town collection for a food basket to be sent to a destitute family at Christmas, then had sent the mother of the family a silk dress because "she has no money, she has no food. But she's getting food, she's being looked after. But never in her life has she had a silk dress."

The discovery stunned Carter. Ruth recalled that "it was one of the few times I ever saw [him] cry." His father, he came to believe, was not a racist but the product of a particular time and culture that warped the oppressor as well as the oppressed. Carter came to believe that it simply was not possible for a white southerner of Earl Carter's generation to act any differently. According to Lillian Carter, the terms "segregationist" and "integrationist" were not used during Earl Carter's lifetime.

After Earl Carter's death, his eldest son saw him as a decent man who had behaved as humanely as possible within the confines of a restrictive social system. Earl Carter had never objected to his wife's good works; it was Earl Carter's money that paid for the medicine she used to treat her patients. Including the children and spouses of the sharecroppers who worked his land, Earl Carter had had more than 1,500 people economically dependent upon him. When one included the white farmers for whom Earl Carter served as one of Sumter County's economic institutions, that number swelled. A fellow navy officer remembers Carter agonizing about whether he should quit the service and return home: ". . . he'd come from this little town of Plains, Georgia, and it was almost like a medieval idea, that one man, his father, was responsible for the souls in the town of Plains, Georgia. . . . Without his father, those 1,500 people were not going to have any way to live." Looking at the lives Mr. Earl had touched, Carter decided, as he told his sister Ruth, that he wanted to be a man like his father.

Jimmy Carter (center, right) and the other Georgia senators are sworn into office on January 15, 1963. Although Carter began his term as senator with characteristic optimism — he promised to read every piece of legislation that came before him — he soon began to feel that he was not cut out for legislative work.

His mother's pleadings also played a role in Carter's decision to return. Lillian was a strong and independent woman, but business had been Earl's province. It was never discussed at home. Left distraught by Earl's sickness and death, she was unable to cope with handling his financial affairs, and she asked her eldest son to take over the family enterprises.

Carter, his wife, and their three sons — James Earl and Donnel Jeffrey had followed not long after John William — moved into an all-white public housing project in Plains. (Technically, Carter had no assured income at the time.) Carter threw himself into learning and managing the family business with his usual drive. He read, took classes, and sought the counsel of more experienced farmers. The work became a family affair. Although Rosalynn had threatened to leave him if he resigned his commission, she took accounting courses and was soon keeping the books for the business. Carter returned at a crucial point for the family enterprises. Advances in method and technology were transforming agriculture in Georgia. After a rocky first year — Carter had inherited at least $40,000 in outstanding loans and debt, and a drought and resulting bad harvest made it difficult for most people to pay what they owed — the business prospered. Carter kept abreast of de-

Civil rights leader Dr. Martin Luther King, Jr., points the way to the state capitol in Montgomery, Alabama, the final destination of a 1965 freedom march. Next to King is his wife, Coretta, and on his right are Dr. Ralph Bunch and the Reverend Ralph Abernathy.

velopments in the field and invested profits in improvements for the Carter operations. Most of the Carter land was used for the cultivation of peanuts; by the 1970s, peanuts were Georgia's leading cash crop, and Carter's Warehouse and associated enterprises were grossing $2.5 million per year. By the middle of his presidency, Carter's personal net worth exceeded $1 million.

Prosperity and the family name virtually ensured that Carter would become involved in community affairs. He became a deacon at the Plains Baptist Church and a Bible instructor, raised funds to build a town swimming pool, and joined the community school board. Although isolated and rural, Plains was affected by the same social changes that were taking place in the rest of the South. In 1954 the Supreme Court of the United States ruled in *Brown v. Board of Education of Topeka*, Kansas, that segregated schools violated the Constitution. "Separate but equal" black educational institutions, as had been the norm in the South (the schools were in fact invariably inferior to their white counterparts), were now illegal. School systems were ordered to desegregate "with all deliberate speed."

As it applied to the alacrity with which southern educational systems moved to desegregate, deliberate proved to be the operative word. When Carter joined the school board in 1956, Plains had not yet acted to desegregate. Carter was proud of his relatively enlightened racial views, yet he remained blind to much of the reality of segregation in his hometown. "It seems hard to believe now," he wrote in *Why Not the Best?*, "but I was actually a member of the county school board for several months before it dawned on me that white children rode buses to their schools and black students still walked to theirs." This realization, however, did not lead him to press for desegregation but only for buses to carry the black students to their schools. He also advocated an upgrading of black educational facilities. Carter voted in favor of awarding sick pay and raises to white teachers while denying the same benefits to black instructors, and he supported scheduling the opening of the black school later than the white

The Plains Baptist Church, where the Carter family and most of the white population of the Georgia hamlet worshiped. Although Carter's civil rights record as a senator was mediocre, in 1964 he did vote to allow blacks to worship alongside whites for the first time in the Plains Baptist Church.

Jimmy Carter announces his candidacy for governor at the state capitol in Atlanta, Georgia, on April 3, 1966. A relative unknown, Carter came in third in the Democratic primary behind segregationist candidate Lester Maddox, who finished first, and Ellis Arnall.

school so that the black children would be available as field hands at harvesttime. (Historians Bruce Mazlish and Edwin Diamond state in their perceptive *Jimmy Carter: An Interpretive Biography*, "The prevailing argument in defense of the sorry state of the blacks' segregated schools was 'If we educate the Negro, then who will work the farms?' ") It is a measure of the intransigence of white southern attitudes at the time that Carter's support for improvement of black facilities earned him something of a reputation as a maverick and an integrationist.

Carter found that he enjoyed politics. Having achieved success in business and as a community leader, it is not surprising that he turned his attention to state office. In 1962 a new seat was created in the Georgia state senate that represented Sumter and two other counties, and Carter decided to run for it. When the ballots were counted, Carter lost by a narrow margin to Homer Moore, the chosen candidate of the Quitman County political organization. Carter characterized his campaign as "amateurish," but on election day he acted like a savvy political professional. Familiar with the Quitman County faction's reputation for ballot-box stuffing and other election fraud, he stationed observers at the polls on election day. Carter's men counted 333 people voting in Quitman County that day, but 422 ballots were tallied there, just enough of them marked for Homer Moore to give him the victory.

Carter was never one to accept defeat easily, but the fraud in Quitman County enraged him. When local journalists proved uninterested in pursuing the story, Carter enlisted the aid of an Atlanta reporter, John Pennington, who wrote a series of articles on the rigged election. He also hired the services of Charles Kirbo, a prominent Atlanta attorney. Together the three men succeeded in having the results of the tainted election invalidated. In the write-in election that followed, Carter won by more than 700 votes (out of 5,000 cast).

As a state senator Carter compiled an undistinguished record. His admiration for Rickover's detail-oriented management style had led him to make a campaign promise that he would read every piece of legislation that came before the legislature, a pledge that he soon regretted, although he gamely took a speed-reading course in order to fulfill it. During Carter's two terms in the senate — he was reelected in 1964 — civil rights was the dominant issue in the South. Under the leadership of the Reverend Martin Luther King, Jr., and others, the determination of blacks to achieve the rights and freedoms promised them under the Constitution was expressed in sit-ins, marches, and other forms of nonviolent protest. For the most part Carter remained quiet on the issue, although he did vote in favor of abolishing the literacy test used to deny blacks their right to vote. At home he was one of the few Plains residents to vote to allow blacks to attend church services at the Plains Baptist Church.

Carter's personality made him ill suited for legislative work, in which personal relationships and the ability to bargain and compromise are paramount. He was again a loner, with few friends among his fellow state senators. He made few speeches and was responsible for very few pieces of legislation.

Despite his mediocre record and the advice of aides such as Kirbo, Carter decided to run for governor in 1966. His chief drawback was his lack of recognition around the state. Few voters had heard of the two-term Democrat from Sumter County; his record offered few reasons why they should vote for him. Indeed, few knew whether he was a liberal or conservative. Carter himself believed he was beyond such labels, that he was "a more complicated person than that." Regardless, many voters were won over by Carter's apparent integrity and honesty as well as his pledges to fight against the special interests that benefited from much of the legislation passed in the state legislature. He seemed to offer a middle-of-the-road alternative to the other Democratic candidates, the liberal Ellis Arnall, whose best days in politics were deemed to be behind him, and Lester Maddox, an unreconstructed racist who would win fame for distributing ax handles to patrons of his restaurant for use on any black who might attempt to enter the eatery.

Although my efforts to establish a viable business were almost a full time job, other opportunities arose for involvement in public affairs.
—JIMMY CARTER

The governor of Alabama, George Wallace, surrounded by state highway patrolmen, confronts Deputy Attorney General Nicholas Katzenbach (extreme left) at the University of Alabama in 1963. The confrontation and subsequent rioting were the result of Wallace's refusal to allow black students to attend the racially segregated school.

Carter came in third in the primary; Maddox won the primary and the general election that followed. In his memoirs Carter allowed that the experience was "extremely disappointing"; his mother recalled that he "cried like a baby." He had lost 22 pounds during the campaign, and he was more than $15,000 in debt. Friends recall Carter being extremely depressed in the aftermath of the election, and there is no doubt the defeat provoked in him a profound spiritual and psychological crisis.

Its resolution occurred when Carter underwent the spiritual experience referred to as being "born again," meaning that he made a conscious decision to renew the devotion to Christian values he adopted when he was baptized and to dedicate his life to the teachings of Jesus Christ. Some believe Carter's spiritual renewal was sparked during a walk in the woods with his sister Ruth, who by this time had achieved prominence as an evangelist and faith healer. Ruth Carter Stapleton (her married name) had always been Carter's closest sibling, and he confided in her the frustration he was feeling with his life. She spoke to him of the joy and serenity her religious faith had brought her and asked whether he would sacrifice all he had for Christ. He responded affirmatively but balked when she asked if that included politics. Stapleton recalls that when she told her brother he would never find tranquillity if that were the case, he broke down and wept.

Shortly afterward he volunteered for a mission as a Baptist lay preacher and spent much of the next year proselytizing in Massachusetts and Pennsylvania. Carter described his experience to Mazlish and Diamond as the gaining of "a new sense of release and assurance and peace with myself and a genuine interest in other people that I hadn't experienced before." He believed that his spiritual rebirth enabled him to focus on how he could help others rather than on his own concerns.

No sooner had Carter recovered from his loss than he began planning for the 1970 gubernatorial campaign. In the next 3 years he made nearly 2,000 speeches around the state and planned his electoral strategy. Sensing that his rival for the Democratic nomination would be former governor Carl "Barefoot" Sanders, by Georgia standards a liberal with close ties to the wealthy Atlanta political establishment, Carter planned to make use of the resentment of working-class and rural Georgians, who Carter believed felt excluded from government. He dubbed Sanders "Cuff Links" Carl and portrayed him as a friend of special interests who had profited from his years in government while painting himself as a friend of the "little people" and working class.

Carter did not hesitate to make use of the racial fears of white southerners. "I do not consider myself a liberal," he declared, acutely aware that the term connoted support for civil rights. He characterized himself as "basically a redneck" and a "white man's candidate," adding that he expected support from "the people who voted for George Wallace for president and the ones who voted for Lester Maddox." (Wallace, the governor of Alabama, had defied court orders for desegregation and proclaimed "Segregation today, segregation tomorrow, segregation forever!" In the 1968 presidential election he had stunned many political observers with his surprisingly strong showing in the Democratic presidential party primaries and then as a third-party candidate.) Carter accused Sanders of having refused to invite Wallace to speak in Georgia in order to appease "a group of ultra-liberals, particularly those in Washington."

> *I was going through a state in my life then that was a difficult one. I had run for governor and lost. Everything I did was not gratifying.*
> —JIMMY CARTER

Carter and Dr. Martin Luther King, Sr., clasp hands during a 1976 political rally in Atlanta. When Carter was elected governor in 1970, he made racial equality a major part of his political agenda.

Carter viewed such tactics less as old-style Southern race baiting than as an exercise in practical politics. His first goal was to get himself elected; then he could exercise the kind of leadership that would enable Georgia to move forward. In his standard campaign speech he asserted that "Georgia people are conservative, but their conservatism does not mean racism . . . that we hide our heads in the sand and refuse to recognize that changes are inevitable . . . that we are callous or unconcerned about our fellow man. . . . Georgians are conservative. So am I."

No matter what terminology was used to characterize Carter's campaign tactics, they were effective, and he had become an extremely formidable candidate. Four years earlier his shyness had prevented him from impressing potential contributors, but in the meantime he had learned to capitalize on his strengths. Still an indifferent orator without charisma, Carter discovered that he could be extremely persuasive in small groups, where his quiet determination and intelligence played to best advantage. His newfound style led a longtime adversary to deem him "as good a campaigner as anybody you've seen in the last 25 or 30 years in politics. One-on-one, he's probably as convincing as anybody

I've ever seen." The results of the election verified the wisdom of Carter's strategy. He won the primary, secured the Democratic nomination, and won the election that followed, garnering 60 percent of the vote to easily defeat his Republican rival.

Once in office Carter took a different tone. "The time for racial discrimination is past," he announced in his inaugural address, and he infuriated white racists by insisting that a portrait of Martin Luther King, Jr., be hung in the state capital. His primary efforts as governor consisted of trying to reorganize the state government. To some it seemed that the Georgia state government existed only as a machine for the distribution of political patronage. The legislature sat, on the average, for only 45 days a year; most of its work seemed to consist of the awarding of lucrative government contracts that benefited the cronies and supporters of one legislator or another. Carter promised to bring efficiency to government, and to a certain extent he was successful. He reduced the number of state agencies from 300 to 22, although critics charged that this did not represent a reduction in the size of government, only a regrouping under different headings. The reorganization enabled him to cut the budget without significantly reducing services, and when he left office in 1974 he was able to boast of a budget surplus of $13 million. Carter also enacted several environmental and conservation measures and overhauled the state's social services bureaucracy. Overall, he was most successful in areas where he could achieve results by virtue of executive action, less successful in shepherding programs through the legislature. Critics complained that Carter lacked a clear vision of what he wanted to achieve in his administration; he was less a leader than a manager. Others were puzzled by their inability to label him as either a liberal or conservative. Supporters embraced Carter's moderation and asserted that the time for ideologues was past. What was needed now, they believed, and what Carter offered, was sound management, fiscal prudence, and pragmatic solutions for complex problems.

Georgians never again want a Governor who will use the tremendous power and prestige of the office for his personal wealth.
—JIMMY CARTER
campaigning in 1970

4

Purging Corruption: The People's Aardvark

Georgia state law prevented governors from serving consecutive terms, but Carter didn't mind. He had already set his sights on another position; he had considered running for the presidency as early as 1972. It was an ambition that seemed unlikely to be fulfilled. No president had been elected from a southern state since Zachary Taylor, the Virginian hero of the Mexican War, in 1848. Carter had never held national office and was virtually unknown outside of Georgia.

As Carter's term as governor drew to an end, however, his candidacy began to appear a more worthwhile gamble. On August 8, 1974, Richard Nixon became the first president of the United States to resign his position. Less than two years earlier Nixon had won one of the most smashing electoral victories in American history. He had polled nearly 18 million more votes than his Democratic rival,

Jimmy's Running for What?
—Reg Murphy's headline for a column in the Atlanta *Constitution*

President-elect Jimmy Carter waves to photographers as he boards Air Force One in June 1976. Carter successfully presented himself as a people's candidate, an honest and unpretentious man who felt more comfortable in cardigan sweaters, blue jeans, and work boots than in formal presidential attire.

A portable radio and an electronic news display atop Allied Chemical Tower in New York City's Times Square relate the historic news of President Richard Nixon's resignation on August 8, 1974. Disillusioned by the corruption of Nixon's Republican administration brought to light by the Watergate scandal, voters looked to the Democrats — and Jimmy Carter — for honest government.

George McGovern, and won every state but Massachusetts. His total of 521 electoral votes was only 2 shy of the highest total ever recorded, by Franklin Roosevelt in 1936. Nixon's downfall began on the night of June 17, 1972, when a number of Cuban emigrés were apprehended breaking in to the Democratic party's national headquarters, located in the Watergate hotel and office complex in Washington, D.C. Subsequent investigation revealed that the burglars had earlier wiretapped the phones in the Democratic headquarters and had been hired by Nixon's campaign organization, the Committee to Reelect the President.

News of the break-in certainly did Nixon little harm in the 1972 election, and for a time it seemed destined to be remembered as nothing more than an unsavory campaign "dirty trick." Nixon claimed the break-in was the work of overzealous and misguided campaign workers. He announced that White House counsel John Dean had conducted a complete investigation demonstrating that "no one in the White House staff, no one in this administration presently employed, was involved in this very bizarre incident."

Two reporters from the *Washington Post*, Bob Woodward and Carl Bernstein, had their doubts about Nixon's version of affairs and continued to pursue the story. They discovered, in their own words of October 10, 1972, that the Watergate break-in was just one incident in a "massive campaign of political spying and sabotage conducted on behalf of President Nixon's reelection." Subsequent articles in the *Washington Post* and other newspapers and a congressional investigation revealed that the Nixon campaign had collected millions of dollars in illegal contributions, bugged the phones and ordered covert surveillance of prominent Democrats, planned to sabotage the Democratic convention, and even proposed firebombing the offices of a liberal think tank. All this was the work of a "special investigative unit" established in the White House at Nixon's behest. Labor leaders, congressmen, members of student organizations, journalists, writers, actors, and others who opposed Nixon's policies were placed under surveillance by the FBI or had their taxes audited by the IRS, as the Nixon administration attempted, in the words of John Dean, who eventually decided to cooperate with the Congressional investigation, "to use the available federal machinery to screw our political enemies."

The Senate's Select Committee on Presidential Campaign Activities established that Nixon and virtually every top White House official not only had known about the Watergate break-in and related activities but had participated since its discovery in a cover-up designed to conceal their complicity. This cover-up provoked a constitutional crisis when Nixon defied the demands of special prosecutor Archibald Cox that he turn over tape recordings made of White House discussions concerning Watergate. With most of his former top aides under or facing indictment (some even were cooperating with the investigation), Nixon responded in October 1973 by firing Cox and attempting to abolish the office of the special prosecutor. Shortly afterward, an outraged Congress voted to begin considering articles of impeachment against Nixon. The Watergate affair dragged on until the following summer, when the Supreme Court ruled that Nixon had to relinquish the tapes. Facing almost certain impeachment and conviction, Nixon resigned in shame.

Tourists at the Carter campaign headquarters — an old train depot — in Plains shortly after Carter's election in 1976. Carter's election as president put the tiny Georgia town on the map.

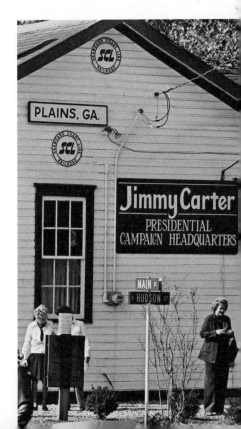

A Jimmy Carter supporter at the 1976 Democratic National Convention in New York City holds a sign that bears two important symbols of the Carter campaign — the peanut, which is a reference to the candidate's successful peanut farm in Plains, and the unmistakable Carter smile.

Watergate marked the end of an extremely turbulent time in American history. The civil rights movement had forced many Americans to question their country's commitment to justice for all its citizens, black or white. The Vietnam War divided the country into those who believed the United States had a moral commitment to defend its allies and fight against communism and those who believed that the massive suffering in Vietnam as a result of the war made U.S. involvement immoral. The violence that seemed to pervade American life in the 1960s and early 1970s — political assassinations, widespread rioting in urban areas, a rising crime rate — led Americans to ask whether there was something fundamentally wrong with their society. The pattern of cynical and criminal behavior by the highest officials in the land uncovered in the Watergate scandal left Americans distrustful of their government. Watergate ushered in a period of profound disillusionment, "a veritable floodtide of disenchantment," in the words of pollster Louis Harris.

This post-Watergate disillusionment paved the way for the success of Carter's candidacy. If Americans no longer trusted those who governed them — and polls indicated they did not — then Carter's paltry 2 percent national recognition factor was no longer the immense drawback that it seemed. It allowed him to campaign as an "outsider" at a time when all politicians were suspect. His not having held national office benefited him in the same way, whereas more established politicians had to overcome the general distrust of anyone associated with "that mess in Washington." The fact that Carter held no office at all after 1974 also helped him by enabling him to campaign full-time.

Democratic pollster Pat Caddell believed that the image Americans had of themselves and their country could be "summed up in one central belief: America was a special place. . . . Americans were a chosen people, different from others." Carter and his strategists, Hamilton Jordan and Jody Powell, recognized that although Americans had been shaken in that belief, they still wanted to feel that way about themselves again. Caddell believed that in 1976 the electorate would be driven by the desire for change and the wish for a return to "basic values." Finally, Carter's strategists all agreed that Watergate ensured that the election would turn less on issues than on character. Powell felt that the majority of the electorate only thought about national politics "once every 4 years for 15 minutes or so." In 1976, he was certain, voters would be concerned more with whether a candidate was a man they could trust than with his positions.

As a candidate, Carter was able to embrace all these themes. His small-town, rural upbringing seemed to harken back to a more innocent, mythical America, a land of virtuous gentleman farmers that was devoid of such ugly modern problems as drug addiction and urban slums. He was photographed

Presidential candidate Jimmy Carter and President Gerald Ford fold their arms and grin as they wait for technical difficulties to be corrected at their 1976 televised debate in Philadelphia. Carter came across better in person than he did on television, where he frequently seemed stiff and nervous.

The Carter clan at the 1976 Democratic National Convention in New York City. From left to right are Jimmy's mother, Lillian; his daughter, Amy, and his son John William, also known as Jack; Jimmy himself and his wife, Rosalynn; son Donald William, called Jeff, and his wife, Annette.

draining a pond on his farm, tending to his peanuts, and hosting a fish fry for his staff and campaign reporters. His religious beliefs appealed to the growing born-again movement in America and helped reassure those concerned that their next president be a man of character. Voters dismayed by the hypocrisy and deceit of the Nixon era responded positively to Carter's assurance that he would never lie to them, indeed "would rather lose the election, and even my wife, than betray the confidence the American public has in me." He promised that his government "would be as filled with love as are the American people."

Powell believed that the traditional classifications of conservative and liberal would be less meaningful in the 1976 election, and Carter's lack of a defined ideological stance served him well. Carter was perceived as a moderate, which in light of doctrinaire liberal George McGovern's crushing 1972 defeat proved to be a blessing. He worked hard to present the image of a populist, a "man of the people," who promised to overhaul the "bloated unmanageable bureaucracy" in Washington and also spoke of government's responsibility to "make a concerted effort to understand people who are poor, black, speak a foreign language, who are not well-educated, who are inarticulate, who are timid, who have some monumental problem." The populist also reminded voters, with slight exaggeration, that he was a "physicist," at home with technology and science. Unlike past presidential candidates, Carter was often photographed informally, wearing blue jeans, and he was fond of quoting the lyrics of singer Bob Dylan, whose work, he said, had taught him much about social justice. While campaigning he stayed in the homes of supporters rather than in luxury hotels.

Carter's greatest advantage was that he was a Democrat seeking to succeed a Republican administration involved in the worst political scandal in American history. The Democrats, one prominent party official said, "could run an aardvark this year and win." That seemed to make winning the nomination Carter's most important task. Carter was one of the first candidates to realize the importance of changes in Democratic party rules designed to make the nominating process more receptive to popular opinion and local participation, changes that made the state primaries even more important. Previously, it had been possible for a candidate to win the nomination without entering any primaries, as Hubert Humphrey had done in 1968, but the new rules made such a scenario unlikely. Whereas candidates such as Senator Fred Harris of Oklahoma, Senator Birch Bayh of Indiana, Senator Henry Jack-

A campaign poster is displayed on Main Street, Plains, Georgia. In 1976, when this photograph was taken, the population of Plains numbered 683, and a local boy named Jimmy Carter was about to become president of the United States.

The farmer who would be president, Jimmy Carter, scales a mountain of peanuts in his Plains warehouse in 1976.

son of Washington, Congressman Morris Udall of Arizona, Senator Frank Church of Idaho, Governor Edmund "Jerry" Brown of California, and Wallace of Alabama carefully selected which states they would spend time and money in, Carter, the self-proclaimed populist, vowed to take his candidacy to the people in as many locations as possible. He campaigned in 30 of the 31 states where primaries were held, missing only West Virginia. Whereas other candidates dismissed the Iowa caucuses — party meetings held at locations throughout the state to determine the extent of popular support for the various candidates — as unimportant, Carter recognized that the person-to-person campaigning required in Iowa was ideally suited for him. Iowa also had the advantage of being a farm state. Carter's unexpected victory in Iowa, the first contest of the primary season, gave his campaign recognition and momentum; when he followed it with a victory in the first primary, held in the small New England state of New Hampshire, the snickering question "Jimmy who?" from political pundits and wags became less audible. Carter went on to win 17 primaries, securing enough delegates to win the party's nomination on the first ballot at its July convention. Polls taken after his primary victories showed that Carter appealed to virtually every category of Democrat — liberal, conservative, moderate, working-class, black.

His Republican opponent, Gerald Ford, left his party's convention trailing Carter by more than 30 points in the polls. Ford had joined the Nixon administration when he was appointed to replace Vice-president Spiro Agnew after Agnew's resignation on the eve of his trials for tax evasion and graft. Ford had acceded to the presidency upon Nixon's resignation. Genial and good-natured, Ford sought to assure Americans that the "long national nightmare" of Watergate was behind them, but he provoked controversy and severe criticism by granting Nixon a pardon for any crimes he may have committed while in office.

Secure in his lead, Carter wished to make character and Watergate the central themes of the campaign. He criticized Ford repeatedly for the pardon while reminding voters that he would run an "open government." Ford responded with familiar but stale criticisms — Carter, he said, was vague on the issues and lacked clear positions. "He wavers, he wanders, he wiggles, and he waffles," Ford charged. Although Carter did have specific plans he wished to implement — reduction of unemployment and inflation, an amnesty for Vietnam War draft resisters, a foreign policy based on human rights and dedicated to ending torture and oppression in other nations, nonproliferation of nuclear arms, reduction of U.S. military forces abroad — Ford's charges brought results. Carter also harmed himself by granting an interview to *Playboy* magazine (a monthly publication often criticized for what some consider its exploitation and degradation of women) in which he revealed that he had looked upon a lot of women with "lust in [his] heart," adding that his religious beliefs considered this as much a sin as committing adultery. When the interview appeared in late September, some praised Carter's honesty and openness of character; others questioned the propriety of his answering questions in a magazine such as *Playboy* and wondered if he was flaky. The "weirdo factor," as Hamilton Jordan called it, hurt Carter in the polls.

Carter's lead diminished from 20 to 8 points after the first televised debate with Ford, in which he appeared wooden and deferential. Ford continued to gain, but his momentum was slowed when his secretary of agriculture, Earl Butz, told some racial jokes that were repeated in a national magazine. The incumbent president also enhanced his image for bumbling when he foolishly stated in the second debate that there was "no Soviet domination of Eastern Europe." Carter went on the offensive, hammering away at the pardon and the mishandling of the American evacuation of the South Vietnamese capital of Saigon a year earlier. The election was the closest since 1916. Carter won 297 electoral votes to 241 for Ford, and he tallied a majority of less than 2 million votes out of more than 80 million cast.

Watergate . . . had come to a head with the resignation of President Nixon. And Carter was determined to make trust and integrity his major rallying cries to the electorate.
—VICTOR LASKY
Carter biographer

5

Governing on Empty

On his inauguration day, January 20, 1977, Carter and his family surprised onlookers by leaving their automobiles during the motorcade down Pennsylvania Avenue and walking the 1.2 miles from Capitol Hill to the White House. Senator William Proxmire of Wisconsin had suggested to Carter that he walk as a means of encouraging Americans to become more physically fit. Carter had rejected the idea as "rather silly" but then realized that the gesture could serve as powerful populist symbolism, showing Carter's common touch and desire to be close to the people. Such symbolism was prevalent in the early days of the Carter administration. At his inauguration he wore a plain business suit rather than the formal wear favored by his predecessors. At the 11 parties she and her husband attended that evening, Rosalynn wore the same dress she had worn to her husband's 1971 inauguration as governor. Many of the guests at the inaugural balls were the citizens at whose homes Carter and his staff had stayed during the campaign.

We're trying to give Mr. Carter what he wants—a simple, modest, inexpensive inauguration that will involve all the 215 million people in this country.
—BARDYL TIRANA
organizer of the Carter
inaugural jubilee

President Jimmy Carter, First Lady Rosalynn, and their daughter, Amy, lead the inaugural parade down Pennsylvania Avenue in the capital on January 20, 1977. Carter reinforced his populist image when he decided to follow the traditional parade route on foot instead of in the back of an open limousine.

President Jimmy Carter takes the oath of office administered by Chief Justice Warren Burger, as First Lady Rosalynn looks on. A spirit of optimism surrounded the early days of the Carter presidency, as a public that had grown cynical and disillusioned during the Nixon years responded with approval to the new president's idealistic outlook.

A man of relatively simple tastes, Carter did away with some of the more ostentatious reminders of the Nixon years. He ordered the presidential yacht, the *Sequoia*, sold. Key White House staffers arrived for work in their own automobiles rather than chauffeur-driven limousines. The first movie the Carters watched in the White House was *All the President's Men,* which told the story of how *Washington Post* reporters Carl Bernstein and Bob Woodward uncovered the Watergate scandal. Carter styled his first televised address as a fireside chat, Franklin Roosevelt's term for his reassuring radio talks to the American public during the Great Depression, and appeared next to a crackling blaze in the White House library wearing a cardigan sweater. The symbolism was for the most part effective, but transforming programs and proposals into effective policy proved to be a difficult challenge.

The most important positions on Carter's White House staff were filled by Georgians, people the president had worked with before and trusted. Jody Powell became press secretary; Hamilton Jordan acted as White House chief of staff, although he did not use that title until two and a half years into the administration. Carter selected another Georgian, Frank Moore, to serve as congressional liaison. Jack Watson, an Atlanta attorney, agreed to be cabinet secretary and assistant for intragovernmental affairs. Stuart Eizenstat, who had worked for President Lyndon Johnson, was asked to be responsible for preparing legislative proposals and monitoring Congress.

Carter's cabinet selections represented a broader geographic spectrum. While Carter was pondering his choices, Jordan said that he felt it would be a betrayal of Carter's campaign stance as a Washington outsider if such established political figures as Cyrus Vance and Zbigniew Brzezinski received appointments. Considerable embarrassment followed when Vance was asked to be secretary of state and Brzezinski received the cabinet-level position of assistant to the president for national security affairs. Vance became Carter's closest personal friend among his Cabinet members, and Brzezinski became perhaps his most relied-upon adviser. Brzezinski met with the president first thing every morning and at several other times during the course of a typical day. In *Keeping Faith*, Carter says that his desire to "reassure some Americans who did not yet trust a group of southerners to manage the affairs of the country" was a key factor in choosing his cabinet, but he had always been better connected than his campaign rhetoric allowed. For several years prior to his run for the presidency Carter had been a member of the Trilateral Commission, a group of influential industrialists, politicians, and intellectuals from the United States, Japan, and Europe. The commission was funded by Chase Manhattan Bank chairman David Rockefeller; its purpose was to analyze such issues as the decline of the United States as a world power and the future problems of the American economy.

For his major appointments, Carter had gone to . . . traditional Establishment sources—the world of big business, corporate law firms and the Trilateral Commission.
—VICTOR LASKY
Carter biographer

Jimmy and Rosalynn Carter with Vice-president Walter Mondale and his wife, Joan, at one of the many parties that followed the inauguration. Mondale, a former senator from Minnesota, proved to be an unusually active vice-president.

Nine of Carter's top appointees, including Vance, Brzezinski, defense secretary Harold Brown, and Vice-president Walter Mondale, had been founding members of the Trilateral Commission. Other important Carter choices for cabinet and cabinet-level positions included Joseph Califano as secretary of health, education, and welfare, Griffin Bell as attorney general, and Georgia banker and Carter pal Bert Lance as head of the office of management and budget. Carter named two women to his cabinet — Juanita Kreps became secretary of commerce, and Patricia Roberts Harris was appointed secretary of housing and urban development — and he selected the prominent black civil rights activist Andrew Young to be U.S. ambassador to the United Nations. James Schlesinger was tabbed as the first head of the newly created Department of Energy.

The decision to form a separate energy department reflected Carter's belief that establishing a comprehensive energy policy was the most important domestic challenge he faced. As the United States grew ever more advanced technologically, its energy consumption increased. Americans had grown used to thinking of energy — particularly oil — as a limitless resource. For decades huge American oil companies operated freely in foreign countries, earning hefty profits and providing a seemingly inexhaustible supply of petroleum, but gradually those nations — many of them in the Middle East — began taking control of their oil fields. With the 1970s came the realization that oil could be used as a potent political weapon. During the Yom Kippur War between Israel and Egypt, Syria, and Iraq in 1973 and 1974, the Arab oil-producing nations, which controlled two-thirds of the world's petroleum reserves, declared an embargo on the sale of oil to the United States because of its support of Israel. Drastic shortages of gasoline in the United States resulted. Prices rose dramatically, and long lines of cars at gas stations became a common sight. The embargo was lifted after the war, but its success had demonstrated to the Organization of Petroleum Exporting Countries how dependent on foreign oil heavily industrialized Western nations had become. Acting as a cartel, the 13 member nations of OPEC rigidly controlled the supply of oil in order to drive its price upward. The price of a barrel of oil quadrupled in 1973, then more than doubled again later in the decade.

The United States itself produced a large amount of oil, but it was also the world's greatest consumer of petroleum. As Carter saw it, the energy question would only become increasingly important in years to come. It was much more than a matter of convenience for American motorists; the Arab oil embargo had demonstrated that oil could be wielded as a political and economic weapon. Energy policy thus became crucial to the national security of the United States and its allies, some of whom, like Japan, were completely dependent on imports for their energy needs.

Carter believed that the United States was fortunate in that it had the productive capacity to reduce significantly its reliance on foreign imports. The country seemed not to have learned a lesson from the oil embargo, however. At the time of the embargo the United States was importing 35 percent of its oil; that figure had risen to 50 percent over the following 4 years. Because natural gas and oil supplies had always been so abundant and inexpensive in the United States, Americans had never considered how much was used wastefully. Americans were used to overheated office buildings and homes and drove big gas-guzzling automobiles. Carter wished to enact a comprehensive energy program that would encourage domestic production of oil and natural gas, promote conservation of existing energy reserves, and stimulate long-range development of alternative energy sources.

President Carter's chief of staff, Hamilton Jordan, at the national spelling-bee finals in the White House on May 30, 1980. Jordan had recently been cleared of charges that he had snorted cocaine in Manhattan nightclub Studio 54; although he was exonerated, the incident soiled the image of the Carter administration.

White House press secretary Jody Powell waves a collection of Ronald Reagan's budget proposals at a press conference in Washington, D.C., and dismisses them as "preposterous." Powell, a key figure in Carter's political career since 1969, remained one of the commander in chief's most trusted personal and political advisers.

Carter made it clear very early in his administration that he considered energy his number-one domestic priority. His first fireside chat, on February 2, 1977, focused on energy conservation and announced the creation of the energy department. "The amount of energy being wasted which could be saved is greater than the total energy that we are importing from foreign countries," he said. He urged Americans to keep their thermostats at 65 degrees Fahrenheit during the daytime and 55 degrees at night, a simple step that he said "could save half the current shortage of natural gas," which had caused schools and other public buildings in the Northeast to be closed for lack of heating fuel. A day prior to his address Carter had announced that he would present Congress with comprehensive energy legislation within 90 days.

On April 18 Carter again spoke to the American people, announcing that he was sending his energy package to Congress. "The energy crisis has not yet overwhelmed us," he said, "but it will if we do not act quickly. It is a problem we will not be able to solve in the next few years, and it is likely to get progressively worse through the rest of this century. . . . Our decision about energy will test the character of the American people and the ability of the president and the Congress to govern this nation. This difficult effort will be the moral equivalent of war, except that we will be uniting our efforts to build and not to destroy."

The president's energy proposals were based on the premise that past governmental regulation of oil and natural gas prices had discouraged conservation and hindered the development of alternative energy sources. As long as the price of gasoline and oil was kept artificially cheap, there was little incentive to conserve. Similarly, the low prices made it extremely difficult for alternative technologies to compete. The cornerstone of Carter's energy package was the phased deregulation of oil and natural gas prices. Taxes on the windfall profits the oil companies could expect to reap as the benefit of deregulation and increased prices would ensure that a substantial portion of the profits was used to develop new domestic sources of oil and gas as well as alternative technologies, such as coal and solar energy. Other aspects of the legislation provided for tax incentives and other inducements to stimulate conservation and development of domestic energy sources.

The energy program was controversial from the outset. Oil companies and congressmen from oil-producing states such as Texas, Oklahoma, Louisiana, and Alaska applauded deregulation but objected to the windfall profits tax. Representatives

Carter announces the appointment of three new members of his cabinet on December 16, 1976, at a press conference in Plains. From left to right are Andrew Young, ambassador to the United Nations; Zbigniew Brzezinski, national security adviser; and chairman of the Council of Economic Advisers, Charles Schultze.

Carter inspects newly installed solar heating panels on the White House roof in 1979. Soon after he took office Carter gave the burgeoning energy crisis in America number-one priority on his agenda and announced his new energy program, encouraging the development of alternate energy sources such as solar heating.

from coal-producing states — Kentucky, West Virginia, and Pennsylvania, among others — supported those sections of the legislation that encouraged the development and increased use of coal as an energy source, but conservationists opposed the use of coal as harmful to the environment. Automobile manufacturers were interested in keeping the price of gasoline as low as possible. Liberals opposed deregulation and believed money collected from the windfall profits tax could best be spent on social programs. Most difficult of all to convince of the legislation's wisdom were the American people, many of whom remained unpersuaded that the energy situation was indeed of crisis proportions. The public's memory was short; the need for immediate action seemed to diminish with the temporary alleviation of the natural gas shortage and the absence of long gasoline lines. Many Americans were extremely skeptical of the oil companies and believed that the shortages had been intentionally created to drive prices and profits skyward. They saw the most tangible result of Carter's energy legislation as higher prices at the gasoline pumps, increased home-heating bills, and greater profits for the oil companies.

All this meant that the energy program proceeded very slowly through Congress, its journey slowed even further by the extreme complexity of the proposed legislation. The program was embodied in 5 related bills, which Carter wished Congress to consider all at once; the legislation had to pass through 17 separate committees. The proposals concerning oil proved so controversial that Congress decided to consider them at a later date and devote its initial attention to natural gas. Even so, no final decision was reached until October 1978. The legislation almost died several times. A crucial vote to keep the energy program alive passed the House of Representatives by only one vote, 207 to 206, and it had to survive a last-minute filibuster in the Senate aimed at stopping higher natural gas prices resulting from deregulation. Yet, on October 18, 1978, all five bills were passed by both houses of Congress in final form. They had been altered and amended by Congress several times, but Carter considered the program a triumph.

A Minnesota National Guard unit is stationed outside the Koch oil refinery in Pine Bend to protect oil shipments from interference by striking truckers, a harsh reminder of the severity of the energy crisis in America. As the crisis worsened Carter urged Americans to limit their fuel consumption.

Cars line up at a Los Angeles service station on the first day of gas rationing in California, May 1979. Long lines at gas stations were a common sight during the late 1970s, and Americans became increasingly frustrated with what they believed was the Carter administration's inability to deal effectively with the Organization of Petroleum Exporting Countries (OPEC).

He still had his oil program to implement, but his proposals aroused even less enthusiasm than his natural gas program. The same objections were raised to deregulation and the windfall profits tax. Despite a new round of shortages and price increases, the public was tired of hearing about the energy crisis and failed to see how higher prices for the oil companies constituted a solution. Frustrated Americans demanded immediate answers. Carter recognized that his perceived failure to remedy the energy situation was causing a crisis of confidence in his government. He sequestered himself for a week at the presidential retreat at Camp David, Maryland, with members of his staff and cabinet, labor and business leaders, important members of Congress and other politicians, and some of the country's most prominent journalists. He emerged having determined that the public's unwillingness to make temporary sacrifices for the sake of a long-range solution to an extremely complex and critical problem was symptomatic of an even more dangerous trend, resulting from the traumatic national experiences of the 1960s and early 1970s. The country was in a malaise, he believed, brought on in part by the inability of Americans to recognize that as the world changed, so did the United States's role in it. It was time for Americans to start recognizing that there were limits — to American power and influence, to how much gasoline they could consume, to the nation's ability to affect events around the world.

He said as much in a televised speech on July 15, 1979. The nation had suffered a number of serious blows to its confidence, and Carter told his audience, "We were sure that ours was a nation of the ballot, not the bullet, until the murders of John Kennedy, Robert Kennedy, and Martin Luther King, Jr. We were taught that our armies were always invincible and our causes always just, only to suffer the agony of Vietnam. We respected the presidency as a place of honor until the shock of Watergate. We remember when the phrase 'sound as a dollar' was an expression of absolute dependability, until ten years of inflation began to shrink our dollar and our savings. We believed that our nation's resources were limitless until 1973, when we had to face a growing dependence on foreign oil. These wounds are still very deep. They have never been healed." Carter went on to challenge Americans to pull together to solve the energy crisis as a sign of their willingness to end America's malaise, then unveiled his oil proposals, calling for a levy on windfall profits that would be, in his words, the "largest tax ever levied on any industry in the history of the world."

It was too much for Carter to expect an end to the political opposition to his energy program. Congress passed his oil legislation, but with significant alterations. A variable rate was substituted for the flat 50 percent tax on profits he had asked for, and the tax revenues were not earmarked to be used for specific purposes, such as development of new resources or social programs, but went into the general treasury to be used as each new Congress saw fit. Carter had hoped that the tax would be made permanent, but Congress decided that it would expire in 1993 or whenever $227 billion in revenues were collected.

Carter's energy program won him little or no popular support. It pleased neither liberals nor conservatives, oil and gas producers nor consumers, environmentalists nor polluters. Several of the criticisms that would be made of Carter throughout his administration — that he and his staff did not work well with Congress, that he was unwilling to compromise, that he was too bogged down in details to lead effectively — were first heard during the fight to implement his energy program. Yet Carter felt that the struggle had been well worth it. In 1977, 48 percent of the oil used in the United States came from overseas. By 1980 that figure had been reduced to 40 percent. Overall U.S. consumption of oil declined 11 percent during the same period. Although Carter was stung by the criticism and wished that Congress had seen fit to pass his legislation as he had conceived it, he felt that the program that was implemented prepared the United States for a future in which it might no longer be able to rely on foreign oil imports to fuel its economy.

The total energy program did not please anyone completely, but overall it was a good compromise, and I knew that the final result was well worth all our efforts.
—JIMMY CARTER

6

Making Peace

Carter's foreign policy was based on the premise that the power of the United States could and should be used to protect human rights around the world, and he hoped to use American influence to help end torture and oppression abroad. Another critically important tenet of his foreign policy was his belief that the United States should act not simply in response to foreign crises or to advance its strategic interests but to create conditions whereby peace could flourish. No area of the world offered a greater challenge to such a determination than the war-torn Middle East, which from the outset of Carter's presidency was the focus of his peacemaking efforts.

The turmoil in the Middle East revolved around the relationship between Israel and its Arab neighbors. Israel had existed as a nation only since 1948. Before its incarnation as an independent Jewish state, Israel had been known as Palestine and had been home through the centuries to Jews, Christians, and Arabs, most of whom followed the religion of Islam. The Jews revere Palestine as the Holy Land promised them in a covenant with their god, Yahweh, as recounted in the Old Testament of the Bible.

> *It is a new world that calls for a new American foreign policy—a policy based on constant decency in its values and an optimism in our historical vision.*
> —JIMMY CARTER

Egyptian president Anwar Sadat (left), Israeli prime minister Menachem Begin, and President Jimmy Carter join hands on the White House lawn on March 26, 1979, following the signing of the Camp David accords, the historic peace treaty between Egypt and Israel. The tortuous negotiations leading up to the treaty were sustained by Carter's force of will.

Following an Israeli raid, shell-shocked Arab refugees huddle amidst the wreckage of their camp on the Gaza Strip. Since it declared itself an independent Jewish state in 1948, Israel entered into a state of war with its Arab neighbors and its indigenous population of displaced Palestinians. The issue of autonomy for the Gaza Strip's Arab population proved to be a major stumbling block during the Camp David negotiations.

Most of Palestine's Jewish population was driven from the land in the first century A.D. during the harsh rule of the Roman Empire. Christians believe Palestine to be the setting for the life and ministry of Jesus Christ, whom they regard as the son of God and redeemer of mankind. During the Middle Ages, the Christian nations of Europe embarked on holy wars, known as the Crusades, to recover the Holy Land from its Islamic rulers. Muslims (believers in Islam) also consider the Holy Land to be sacred. The Dome of the Rock mosque in Jerusalem, for example, is believed by Muslims to be the site from which the prophet Muhammad ascended into heaven. Muslims gradually came to constitute the vast majority of the population of Palestine, and after the 7th century the land was usually under Arab or Muslim political control.

During the closing decade of the 19th century a movement known as Zionism gathered support among world Jewry. The victims of prejudice, discrimination, and severe repression in virtually every one of the countries in which they had ever settled, the Jews never lost a sense of themselves as constituting a distinct nation. Zionism called for a return of the Jews to Palestine and the establishment of a Jewish state there. Spurred by the government-sanctioned massacres, or pogroms, directed against their communities, Russian Jews began emigrating to Palestine in the late 1800s. Jewish immigration to the Holy Land increased steadily throughout the opening decades of the 20th century. By the outbreak of World War I in 1914 there were 60,000 Jews, 70,000 Christians, and 500,000 Muslims in Palestine.

World War I brought an end to the Ottoman Empire's control of Palestine, and Great Britain received a mandate from the League of Nations, a newly formed international peacekeeping organization, to administer the region. The Balfour Declaration, issued before the war's end by Foreign Secretary Arthur Balfour, promised the support of the British government for the establishment of a Jewish national homeland in Palestine; the League of Nations mandate directed Britain to encourage Jewish settlement. Jewish immigration accelerated — the number of Jews in Palestine reached 250,000 in 1935 — and was met with increased, often violent opposition by the indigenous Arab population. Fierce rioting occurred in 1921 and 1929, and an organized Arab rebellion against British rule began in 1936.

Britain was soon forced to focus its attention on events closer to home. Having already marched into Czechoslovakia and Austria, the German dictator Adolf Hitler invaded Poland on September 1, 1939, bringing an immediate declaration of war from Britain and France. Fearful that the rebellious Arabs might ally themselves with Germany, in 1939 Britain repudiated the Balfour Declaration and announced its intention to restrict and then limit Jewish immigration to Palestine. For Europe's

> *[The Balfour Declaration was] the greatest diplomatic coup of the first world war.*
> —CHARLES WEBSTER
> historian

Jews, however, immigration had taken on a greater urgency, for Hitler's "final solution" — the genocide of all of Europe's Jews — was already in full swing. By the war's end in 1945 more than 6 million of Europe's 10 million Jews had been exterminated. The Jewish communities in Greece, Czechoslovakia, Poland, and Holland were virtually annihilated; many centers of Jewish culture and life were eradicated.

In Palestine, Jews called for independence and an end to Britain's mandate, while the Arabs vowed resistance to the establishment of an independent Jewish state. Militant Jewish groups such as the Irgun and the Lehi carried out terrorist actions designed to drive the British from Palestine. In November 1947 the United Nations voted to partition Palestine into separate Arab and Jewish states. Israel's declaration of independence in May 1948 was followed shortly afterward by war and the invasion of troops from the surrounding Arab states of Egypt, Lebanon, Syria, and Jordan. Israel prevailed over the poorly organized Arab forces and greatly added to its territory. In the process hundreds of thousands of Palestinian Arabs fled or were driven from their homes.

Tension in the area had not diminished in the 28 years between Israel's independence and Carter's inauguration. Israel had fought three more wars with its Arab neighbors, each ending in an Israeli victory and an expansion of its territory. The most significant was the Six-Day War of 1967, which resulted in Israel's wresting control of the Sinai Peninsula and the Gaza Strip from Egypt, the Golan Heights from Syria, and the West Bank of the Jordan River from Jordan. Both the Gaza Strip and the West Bank were inhabited primarily by Palestinian Arabs. Beginning in the 1960s the Palestine Liberation Organization (PLO) and affiliated groups dedicated to the establishment of an independent Palestinian state carried out frequent attacks against Israeli citizens and property. Neither the PLO nor the member states of the Arab League recognized Israel's right to exist, and the Arab League had maintained a continuous declaration of war against Israel since 1948.

Many of Carter's advisers warned him that attempting to bring peace to the Middle East was a no-win proposition. They believed the hostility there was too deeply rooted and that neither side truly wanted peace. Past administrations had tried and failed to gain acceptance of a peace plan; should Carter's efforts not succeed, it would damage the prestige of his presidency. However, Carter believed that there were several factors favoring his peace initiative. Some of the Arab leaders, particularly Egypt's president, Anwar Sadat, were coming to recognize that the cost of war had become prohibitive. Egypt was an extremely poor country, and Sadat realized that money spent on the military could better be used for social and economic programs. For years Egypt had relied on the Soviet Union for economic and military aid, but Sadat had expelled the Soviets in the early 1970s and was now eager for closer relations with the United States.

Israeli prime minister Menachem Begin (wearing glasses) and Egyptian president Anwar Sadat embrace at the conclusion of the Camp David summit, while Carter applauds. Most observers had felt that a treaty between the two bitter enemies was impossible, but persistence and a strong desire for peace proved them wrong.

A satisfied Jimmy Carter presides over the official signing of the Egypt-Israeli peace treaty as Anwar Sadat and Menachem Begin set pen to paper and seal the agreement. The Camp David treaty is considered Jimmy Carter's foremost achievement.

Carter also knew that there was a certain amount of pressure he could bring to bear upon Israel to move it toward peace. The Jewish state had few allies and was extremely dependent upon U.S. foreign aid. The plight of the millions of Palestinian refugees on the West Bank and in the Gaza Strip and Lebanon was receiving increased attention around the world, and the PLO had scored a number of diplomatic triumphs. Although the United States had repeatedly pledged its commitment to Israel's survival, it also needed to maintain cordial relations with the Arab oil-producing states. The supremely tough-minded Israeli leaders were aware the United States had already suffered once from an Arab oil embargo; they also recognized that there was likely a limit as to how much economic hardship the United States was willing to undergo in its friendship for Israel before that relationship cooled. Israel could also hope to profit from peace in the region through an end to the trade embargo the Arab nations had enforced against it.

Carter's concern for human rights made the Palestinian situation of special importance to him. He believed that the Palestinians on the West Bank and in the Gaza Strip should have the right to determine their own future, but he also recognized that the question of Palestinian statehood was tied to Israel's legitimate fears for its safety. Surrounded by hostile Arab states that had engaged it in war 4 times in less than 30 years, Israel worried that a Palestinian state would be used to launch further attacks against it. The Israelis were also concerned that such a state would be dominated by the PLO, whose charter committed it to Israel's destruction. Carter's plan for peace in the Middle East called for some measure of self-determination, short of statehood, for the Palestinians, coupled with an Israeli withdrawal to near its 1967 borders, in exchange for peace.

His first attempts to initiate peace talks failed. When Israeli prime minister Yitzhak Rabin visited the White House in March 1977, Carter characterized their meeting as "an unpleasant surprise." He found Rabin stiff and unyielding, with no constructive suggestions as to how to end the Middle East impasse. An April meeting with Egypt's Anwar Sadat yielded more positive results. No Arab leader had wished to break ranks and discuss peace with Israel, but Sadat expressed willingness to negotiate directly with the Israelis, provided the Palestinian question was addressed. Sadat even conceded the possibility of eventually exchanging ambassadors with Israel. The meeting marked the beginning of what Carter termed "an easy and natural friendship" between the two leaders. He would later say that the Egyptian president was the world leader he admired above all others. Carter was also heartened by his springtime discussions with Hafez al-Assad of Syria and Jordan's King Hussein, who both seemed encouraging, although no Arab leader was yet willing to declare publicly his support for peace.

In April 1977 Menachem Begin succeeded Rabin as prime minister of Israel. During the 1940s, Begin had served as the commander in chief of the Irgun, and during his years in politics he had taken a hardline position on questions of Israel's security. His accession was not likely to make peace any easier to achieve. Begin believed the West Bank to be rightfully part of Israel; he referred to the region by its Biblical names, Judea and Samaria, and would soon reveal himself to be in support of Israeli set-

Sadat had . . . made some slight moves toward moderation, which were already bringing on him severe condemnation from the PLO (Palestine Liberation Organization) and other Arab militants.
—JIMMY CARTER

tlement there. (Any increase in the Israeli settlement on the West Bank made Palestinian self-determination that much more unlikely.) Begin visited Washington in July 1977. Carter found him "quite congenial, dedicated, sincere, deeply religious" and believed their meeting to have been productive, although Begin forcefully reiterated his opposition to a Palestinian state on the West Bank.

No further progress was made until November 9, when Sadat stunned his Arab allies by announcing that he was willing to go to Jerusalem to talk peace with Israel. No Arab leader had ever made an official visit to Israel during nearly 30 years of existence. Begin responded one week later by inviting Sadat to address the Knesset, the Israeli parliament. Sadat's bold gesture infuriated his Arab allies, who considered it an unconscionable betrayal. Syria broke relations with Egypt and declared November 19, when Sadat arrived in Israel, a day of national mourning. Sadat's speech before the Knesset demonstrated anew that the two sides were still far apart, but his courage in going to Israel showed that he was willing to take unprecedented steps for the sake of peace.

Begin, however, was seemingly unable to see that by going to Israel, Sadat had in effect made a significant concession and extended a de facto recognition of Israel's existence. In December, Begin again went to Washington, this time with a plan for autonomy on the West Bank that called for a withholding of Israeli claims of sovereignty over the region for a short period and the granting of a certain amount of control over domestic affairs to the Palestinians. Carter dismissed the plan as inadequate, and no new proposals were forthcoming. Begin continued to encourage Israeli settlement of the West Bank, and he and Sadat began to criticize each other publicly. After meeting with representatives from Israel and Egypt in early 1978, Secretary of State Cyrus Vance told a frustrated Carter that the peace talks were at an end.

Despite the seeming impossibility of his task, Carter continued to try and bring Begin and Sadat together throughout the spring and summer of

Begin reminded me that for 29 years, six Israeli prime ministers had expressed their readiness to go anywhere to meet with any Arab leader in the search for peace.
—JIMMY CARTER
commenting on Begin's
response to Sadat's
announcement that he
would visit Jerusalem

1978. He met twice with Begin and once with Sadat. Although Carter felt that so far Sadat had taken the greater risks for the sake of the negotiations, he believed that each man was sincere in his desire for peace. He made painstaking efforts to portray for each leader the political pressures his counterpart faced and to urge him to see the other side's point of view. His efforts met with frustration. Sadat threatened to announce that Egypt was withdrawing from the peace process, and Begin rejected every suggestion for a possible settlement that Carter made.

With the negotiations at a standstill, Carter decided to make one final attempt. He was willing to admit failure if it was unsuccessful. Believing that Sadat and Begin could resolve their differences if they met face-to-face, Carter invited them to Camp David, the wooded presidential retreat in the Maryland countryside. Both agreed to come. They arrived

The body of Anwar Sadat is carried ceremoniously through the streets of Cairo on October 10, 1981, four days after he was gunned down by Muslim fundamentalist zealots. Carter was saddened by the loss of Sadat; a deep respect had developed between the two men at Camp David.

Arab schoolchildren walk home from school under the gaze of Israeli soldiers on the West Bank. At Camp David, Sadat and Begin agreed to continue discussing Palestinian autonomy for the Israeli-occupied West Bank and Gaza Strip. Throughout the 1980s, however, Israel steadily increased its military presence in the volatile areas.

on September 5. The 3 leaders and their staffs spent the next 13 days together trying to forge an agreement. As previously, Carter found Sadat more open and responsive than his Israeli counterpart. Carter believed that Sadat saw himself as the inheritor of "the mantle of authority from the great pharaohs and was convinced that he was a man of destiny." However, Carter found Begin unyielding and slow to recognize that peace would require cooperation. At times Carter became so frustrated at Begin's intransigence that he accused him, as did Sadat, of being more interested in ensuring that Israel kept all the territory it had gained in the Six-Day War than in obtaining peace.

Carter felt that for a Middle East peace treaty to have any chance for lasting success, it had to be negotiated by the principals themselves, not imposed from without by a third power. He had great hopes that together Begin and Sadat would reach an understanding, but after the two had a bitter argument on the third day they did not meet face-to-face again until the negotiations were almost concluded. That left Carter to act as mediator. He would meet first with one leader or key members of his staff, then with the other, seeking to establish points that the two men could agree upon. Often Carter would make his own suggestions, stating why he felt a particular proposal was fair or explaining to one of the leaders why the other side could never accept a certain point. Much of his time was spent placating Begin or Sadat, seeking to assure the one that the other was not stubborn or unreasonable but concerned with his nation's vital interests and genuinely committed to peace.

The talks almost broke down several times, but on each occasion Carter was able to persuade the two leaders to continue. The chief point of contention remained Israel's refusal to relinquish control of the West Bank. Carter persisted, however, and Begin and Sadat were finally able to reach an agreement on a framework for a peace treaty. It called for Israel's withdrawal from the Sinai Peninsula, which would be returned to Egypt. Begin and Sadat agreed to continue negotiating autonomy for the Palestinians on the West Bank and in the Gaza Strip. Carter spent much of his time during the following months discussing the specific language of the treaty with Begin and Sadat, even traveling to the Middle East to meet personally with the two men. Finally, on March 26, 1979, Begin, Sadat, and Carter met on the south lawn of the White House to sign the Camp David accords, as the historic agreement is often called. Begin and Sadat received the Nobel Peace Prize for their efforts, but Carter deserves equal credit. Although Israel and Egypt were able to make little progress on Palestinian autonomy before Sadat's assassination in October 1981, the two nations stayed at peace throughout the 1980s, and the Camp David accords remain a considerable diplomatic achievement.

For a few hours, all three of us [Carter, Begin, and Sadat] were flushed with pride and good will toward one another because of our unexpected success. We had no idea at that time how far we still had to go.
—JIMMY CARTER

7

Forging a Foreign Policy

The energy crisis and the attempt to bring peace to the Middle East occupied the majority of Carter's time during the first three years of his presidency, but they were by no means the sole issues with which he was concerned. Recession, high unemployment, and inflation required the president's attention. Relations with the Soviet Union proved to be of critical importance, as they had been for every American president since Franklin Roosevelt. Carter hoped to build upon the start Nixon had made toward normalizing relations with the People's Republic of China. The growing unrest in Iran, a valued U.S. ally, would ultimately develop into a full-blown revolution, with unforeseen consequences for the United States. However, perhaps no issue divided opinions as sharply as Carter's policy regarding the Panama Canal.

Connecting the Atlantic and Pacific oceans across the 10-mile-wide Isthmus of Panama, the canal was of inestimable strategic and economic importance.

The Panama Canal fight consumed enormous amounts of White House time and political capital.
—BRUCE MAZLISH
Carter biographer

Carter clasps the hand of Soviet premier Leonid Brezhnev following a June 1979 SALT II (Strategic Arms Limitation Talks) session in Vienna, Austria. Carter began making diplomatic overtures to the Soviet Union immediately upon taking office in 1976; he returned from the Vienna sessions in 1979 with a signed arms-limitation agreement.

On January 10, 1964, the Stars and Stripes is raised by American students at Balboa High School in the Panama Canal Zone, a gesture that outraged Panamanians, who had long resented the U.S.-controlled Canal Zone. President Carter eased the situation in 1978 with a treaty that would return the Canal Zone to Panamanian control in the year 2000.

The United States had secured the rights to build and operate the canal in 1903. At the time Panama was part of the nation of Colombia, but when the Colombian government balked at granting the United States the rights it sought, President Theodore Roosevelt and his advisers encouraged the Panamanians to revolt against Colombia. The U.S. Navy then intervened to prevent Colombia from landing forces to subdue the uprising. Panama declared itself an independent republic on November 3, 1903. Two weeks later the United States signed a treaty with a representative of the Panamanian government, Philippe-Jean Bunau-Varilla, granting it exclusive control, in perpetuity, over the Canal Zone. Within the zone the United States was free to exercise "all the rights, power and authority . . . which the United States would possess and exercise if it were the sovereign of the territory . . . to the entire exclusion of the exercise by the Republic of Panama of any such sovereign rights or authority." Bunau-Varilla's authority to speak for the Panamanian government was dubious at best; he was a Frenchman and had not even visited the area in 18 years. Faced with the withdrawal of U.S. support, Panama had little choice but to ratify the treaty. Over the years American control over the Canal Zone had come to be viewed by patriotic Panamanians as an affront to their nation's sovereignty. In 1964 rioting had resulted when American students had raised the flag of the United States over their school in the zone. Both Lyndon Johnson and Richard Nixon had attempted to negotiate treaties more equitable to Panama, but widespread domestic opposition in the United States had ensured the failure of their efforts.

Carter wished to try again. Panama had been a longstanding friend of the United States, but its continued resentment about the canal threatened to damage irrevocably that amity, as well as U.S. relations with other Latin American and Third World nations. The president saw the canal as a human rights issue and a matter of principle: "a litmus test . . . indicating how the United States, as a superpower, would treat a small and relatively defenseless nation that had already been a close partner and supporter." He also worried that Panama might take independent action to gain control of the waterway, as Egyptian president Gamal Abdel Nasser had done in 1956 with the Suez Canal. Under a new treaty the United States could expect to retain unlimited rights to the use of the canal, but that would not be the case should Panama seize it. Carter regarded the canal as vital to U.S. interests, but his military advisers had informed him that it would be very difficult to defend should Panama move on it. Secretary of Defense Harold Brown believed that it would be much easier to keep the canal in operation by virtue of a "cooperative effort with a friendly Panama" than through the efforts of an "American garrison amid hostile surroundings."

Carter named Sol Linowitz, a corporate lawyer and diplomat with a history of service in Latin America, and Ellsworth Bunker, a longtime State Department official, as the heads of the U.S. negotiating mission to Panama. They were able to reach an agreement with the Panamanians and con-

> *If I could have foreseen early in 1977 the terrible battle we would face in Congress, [on the Panama Treaties] it would have been a great temptation for me to avoid the issue—at least during my first term.*
> —JIMMY CARTER

Construction workers take a break from their labors on the Panama Canal. It took 11 years — from 1903 to 1914 — to build the canal, which cuts across the Isthmus of Panama to connect the Atlantic and Pacific oceans. The massive project was supervised by U.S. military engineers, and most of the manual labor was done by native Panamanians.

cluded two separate treaties. The first called for a return of the Canal Zone to the Panamanians and joint control of the canal's operations until the year 2000, when Panama would assume complete control. The second agreement granted the United States the permanent right to return its troops to the Canal Zone in order to defend the canal against any external threat to its operation.

Presidents before Carter had been able to reach similar understandings about the canal only to have them scuttled in the face of intense domestic opposition. Carter was well aware that securing Congress's ratification would be an even greater achievement. The canal had been an important issue during the 1976 presidential campaign. Ronald Reagan, who had opposed Gerald Ford for the Republican nomination, had earned much applause by telling audiences, "When it comes to the canal, we built it, we paid for it, it's ours and we should tell Torrijos and company [General Omar Torrijos was the head of the Panamanian government] that we are going to keep it." Public opinion in the fall

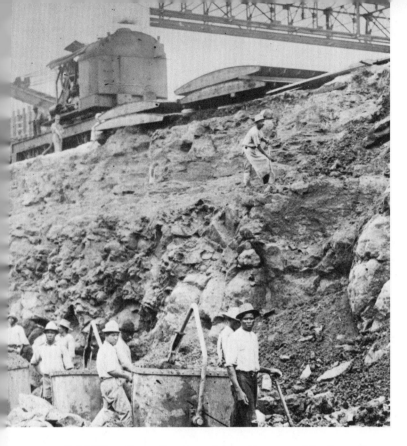

of 1977, when the canal treaties went before Congress, seemed to agree with Reagan. According to polls, only eight percent of the American public favored "giving up" the canal.

A two-thirds majority of the Senate is required for the ratification of foreign treaties. When Carter polled the 100 senators at the time the treaties were signed, in September 1977, only 30 would commit themselves to voting in favor of ratification. While the Senate spent the next 6 months deliberating on the treaties, Carter worked at persuading 37 senators to change their minds. He made numerous phone calls and held many meetings, seeking to convince senators that the treaties were in the nation's best interest. In March 1978 the Senate ratified the first canal treaty; ratification of the second followed a month later. Although Carter believes that the furor over the canal greatly harmed his chances for reelection, he considers the treaties one of his proudest achievements, a tangible affirmation of the United States's commitment to freedom and self-determination during his administration.

At the same time Carter was working to improve relations with Panama and the other Latin American nations, he was also seeking new ties with the People's Republic of China. The United States had broken diplomatic relations with China in 1949, when Mao Zedong and the Chinese Communists had driven the nation's former leader, Chiang Kai-shek, and his government from the mainland to the island of Taiwan. Chiang's government had received huge amounts of economic and military aid from the United States, particularly during World War II. After the Communist victory Chiang established a new government on Taiwan, and the United States continued to provide assistance. Chiang insisted that his regime was the rightful government of all of China, a viewpoint the United States subscribed to for 23 years. Reality belied Chiang's claims; it was soon apparent that he would never fulfill his promise to liberate the mainland from Communist rule. The government of the People's Republic of China, as the mainland state was called, controlled more than one-quarter of the world's population, and throughout the 1960s and 1970s it exerted an increasing influence on world affairs. Realizing that it was no longer diplomatically prudent to ignore the People's Republic, more and more nations withdrew their diplomats from Taiwan. In October 1971 the United States voted to expel the Taiwan delegation and seat instead a mission from the People's Republic as China's representatives.

At about the same time, China's premier, Zhou Enlai, and Nixon's top foreign-policy adviser, Henry Kissinger, were exploring ways to thaw relations between their two countries. China had fallen out with the Soviet Union and was looking to increase its ties to the West, while the United States recognized that a friendship with a powerful Asian nation that shared a border with the Soviet Union could have considerable strategic benefits. Nixon paid a historic visit to China in 1972. While there he and Zhou issued a communiqué that stated there was only one China. The communiqué was an implicit rejection of the claims of Chiang and his successors and put Taiwan on notice that full diplomatic recogni-

tion of the mainland government was only a matter of time. Nevertheless, little progress toward complete normalization of relations between the United States and the People's Republic of China was made in the four years after Nixon's visit.

Carter made full normalization of relations with China one of the early priorities of his presidency. He appointed Leonard Woodcock, who had recently retired as president of the United Automobile Workers union, to be chief of the U.S. liaison office in Beijing, China's capital, and to head the U.S. negotiating efforts. Preoccupied with internal turmoil associated with the deaths of Zhou and Mao and the struggle to determine a successor, the Chinese were initially cautious and unresponsive. But once Deng Xiaoping established himself as the head of the government, the Chinese moved quickly. In November 1978, Carter sent Deng his proposal for normalization, which contained provisions for trade and cultural exchanges as well as diplomatic recognition. Carter's plan also provided for continued ties with Taiwan, although the United States would no longer maintain an embassy there. On December 13, Deng met with Woodcock and agreed to Carter's proposal. January 1, 1979, was designated as the

With a handshake, Carter welcomes Chinese vice-premier Deng Xiaoping to the White House in January 1979. (An interpreter stands between them.) Deng was the first Chinese communist head of state to visit the United States.

date for official normalization, and Deng announced that he would visit the United States at the end of January.

Carter was delighted with Deng's response. There was relatively little domestic opposition to normalization, and Deng's visit was an overwhelming success. Deng's spontaneous exuberance delighted the Carters, and the president felt his discussions with the Chinese leader were forthright and productive, establishing a basis for expanded future ties with the People's Republic. In *Keeping Faith* Carter wrote, "China was one of our few foreign-policy tasks to prove much more pleasant and gratifying than I had expected at the outset of my term."

He was unable to say the same about his dealings with the Soviet Union, which since the end of World War II had engaged with the United States in a worldwide struggle for political and economic influence known as the Cold War. The stockpiling of nuclear weapons by both sides was perhaps the most important consequence of the Cold War; the United States and the Soviet Union each had amassed enough nuclear firepower to destroy the other several times over. During his campaign Carter often spoke of his wish to make the world a safer place by reducing the number of nuclear weapons. This desire manifested itself during his presidency in a resolve to reopen the strategic arms limitation talks (SALT) with the Soviet Union.

The first SALT agreement with the Soviet Union had been reached during the Nixon presidency. Less than three weeks into his own administration, Carter expressed his desire to resume negotiations on nuclear disarmament in a letter to the Soviet Union's leader, Leonid Brezhnev. Conservatives in the United States used the so-called missile gap between the two nations — according to this view, the Soviet Union enjoyed a huge advantage in nuclear weapons — to justify calls for an increased American military buildup and opposition to any nuclear arms limitation agreement. Carter was not convinced of the missile gap's existence, believing that the United States's nuclear stockpile was sufficient for any legitimate defense needs. His examination of the nuclear inventory of both nations persuaded him that although the Soviets possessed more missile launchers and their weapons had more explosive power, this advantage was offset by the greater accuracy of the American nuclear missiles and the diversity of the three-pronged — submarine, land, and air — American nuclear arsenal. (The Soviet Union owned virtually no nuclear bombers.) The United States also had more total nuclear warheads. Carter also recognized that in calculating its vulnerability to nuclear attack the Soviet Union considered not only American weapons but also those possessed by Great Britain and France, both longtime allies of the United States.

Brezhnev's first response to the reopening of disarmament talks was cool, but Carter and his emissaries — Vance, Brzezinski, and Paul Warnke, who was head of the Arms Control and Disarmament Agency — continued to put forward new proposals to Anatoly Dobrynin, the Soviet ambassador to the United States, and Andrei Gromyko, the Soviet foreign minister. Carter had a twofold strategy. He hoped to use SALT II to place overall limits on the construction of nuclear weapons, then use a second agreement, SALT III, as an instrument for the actual reduction of nuclear stockpiles. After more than two years of intense negotiations, the Americans and Soviets reached tentative agreement on a treaty setting specific ceilings on the amount of nuclear weapons each country could possess. Carter and Brezhnev met at a summit conference in Vienna, Austria, in June 1979 to finalize details. The two men got along well personally. News reports had portrayed the aging Soviet leader — Brezhnev was nearly 71 at the time — as ailing and infirm, but Carter was impressed by Brezhnev's vigor and his control of the Soviet delegation. Carter was also reassured about the summit's prospect for success when at their first meeting Brezhnev said to him, "If we do not succeed, God will not forgive us." Brezhnev indirectly confirmed the wisdom of Carter's China policy by repeatedly referring to his concern about the consequences of the normalization of Sino-American relations for the Soviet Union.

I went over the complete inventory of U.S. nuclear warheads, which is really a sobering experience.
—JIMMY CARTER

Carter returned to Washington with a signed arms agreement, but he had felt from the outset that securing the Senate's ratification would be equally, if not more, difficult than reaching an understanding with the Soviet Union's negotiators. As with the Panama Canal treaties, a simple majority in the Senate would not be sufficient to ratify. Carter needed a two-thirds vote, and quite a few of the Republican senators who had defied their party to vote in favor of the canal treaties had already informed him that they could not do so again to support SALT II. The administration organized a massive lobbying campaign in favor of ratification — one that, in Carter's words, "made the Panama Canal treaties effort pale into comparative insignif-

Carter and Brezhnev sign the SALT II treaty on June 18, 1979, in Vienna, Austria. The treaty imposed limits on the manufacture of nuclear weapons, but the Soviet invasion of Afghanistan in 1979 and the subsequent rise of anti-Soviet sentiment in the United States effectively ruined any chance of the treaty being ratified by the Senate.

icance" — but SALT II never even came up for a vote. In December the Soviet Union invaded Afghanistan. Recognizing that the invasion had unleashed a torrent of anti-Soviet sentiment, Carter asked that the Senate postpone its consideration of SALT II, while pledging that the United States would continue to abide by its provisions. Carter hoped that the Senate would be able to consider the treaty at a more propitious time, but Iran and the hostage crisis came to occupy the majority of his attention. Ronald Reagan made opposition to SALT II a theme of his presidential campaign in 1980, and after his election efforts to ratify the agreement were shelved, though both countries adhered, for the most part, to SALT II's terms.

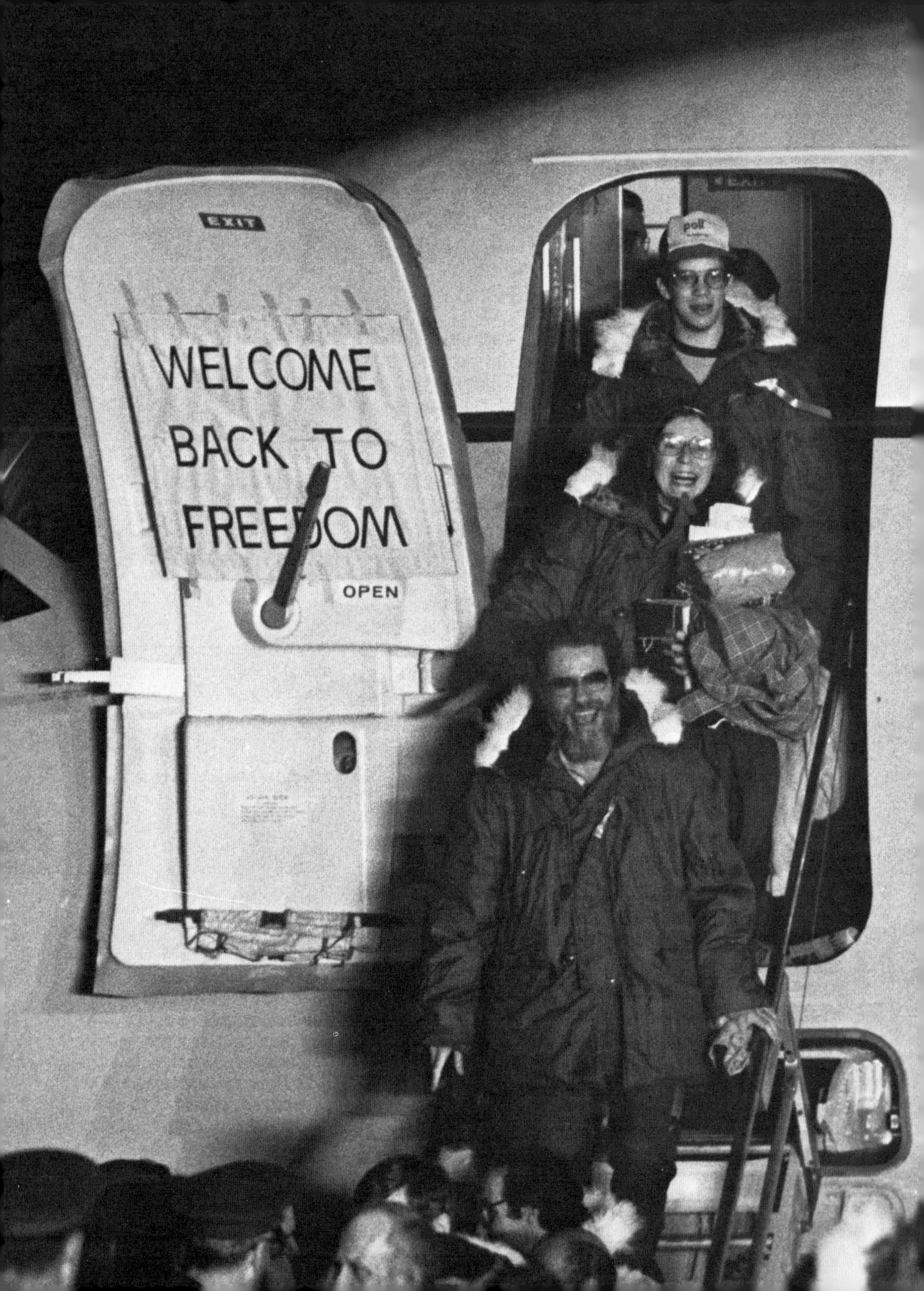
EXIT
WELCOME
BACK TO
FREEDOM
OPEN

8

Gaining Everything

Iran dominated the last year of the Carter presidency. The United States's difficulties there predated the hostage crisis. Iran had been an American ally since the close of World War II, valued for its vast oil reserves and as a buffer against Soviet expansionism in the Persian Gulf region. Over the years the United States poured billions of dollars in military and financial aid into Iran. When Iran's monarch, Shah Mohammed Reza Pahlavi, was ousted in 1953 by Mohammed Mossadeq — a longtime opponent of the Pahlavi monarchy who had nationalized Iran's foreign-owned oil industry — the Central Intelligence Agency (CIA) engineered a coup that restored the shah to his throne. The CIA then funded and trained the shah's new secret police force, *Sazman-e Ettela'at Va Amniyat-e Keshvar.* The words translated from Farsi to English as Organization of State Intelligence and Security, but most people referred to the secret police force by its acronym, SAVAK. The shah used SAVAK to establish one of the world's most repressive regimes. According to a CIA official who served in both nations,

> *We have no intention, neither ability nor desire, to interfere in the internal affairs of Iran.*
> —JIMMY CARTER

On January 21, 1981, elated American hostages disembark at the Rhein-Main Air Base in West Germany following their release from captivity in Iran. Carter spent much of his final year in office bringing about the release of the hostages.

Jimmy Carter and his brother, Billy, enjoy some barbecued chicken at Billy's service station in Plains in September 1976. The hard-drinking and eccentric Billy, a self-professed "good ole boy," would eventually become an irritating thorn in the president's side. Billy died on September 26, 1988, of pancreatic cancer.

SAVAK was more powerful and fearsome in Iran than the KGB was in the Soviet Union. By the 1970s there were more than 60,000 SAVAK agents operating in Iran, answerable only to the shah himself. Using informants at every level of Iranian society, SAVAK imprisoned and tortured thousands of Iranians it suspected of opposing the shah's regime. A casual conversation overheard by a SAVAK informer or possession of proscribed literature was enough to land an Iranian in one of SAVAK's 6,000 jails. Independent political parties and labor unions were banned. The shah exercised virtually unlimited political power, ruling by imperial decree. Amnesty International, a group dedicated to ending political oppression, reported in 1975 "that no country in the world has a worse record in human rights than Iran."

Iran prospered economically under the shah, but the introduction of Western and secular influences that accompanied the economy's modernization offended large segments of the devoutly Muslim population. Despite SAVAK's ruthlessness, opposition to the shah's autocratic rule mounted, much of it led by Muslim clergymen. The Ayatollah (a religious title meaning "miraculous sign of God") Ruhollah Khomeini was the most important of these Islamic fundamentalist leaders. The shah ordered Khomeini deported in late 1964, but while in exile in Turkey, Iraq, and France the ayatollah continued to denounce the shah and call for the establishment of an Islamic republic based on the precepts of Islam's sacred text, the Koran. Tapes of Khomeini's speeches and sermons were smuggled into Iran and circulated among his supporters. Other opponents of the shah pressed for democratic reforms, such as the introduction of a Western parliamentary system. Unrest in Iran increased during the early days of the Carter administration. Several enormous antigovernment demonstrations turned into massacres when the shah's troops fired upon the unarmed protesters. When 400 people died in a fire in a movie theater in Abadan in August 1978, rumors that SAVAK had set the blaze led to rioting throughout the country. A general strike followed, paralyzing the economy, and hundreds of thousands of Iranians took to the streets to demonstrate. From Iraq and then France, Khomeini called for "death to the shah." The ayatollah stressed the U.S. role in supporting the shah's rule, thus much of the rage expressed toward his government was also directed at the United States for its support of the shah's brutal regime. Khomeini denounced the shah as "the American snake whose head must be smashed with a stone."

Carter seems to have been misguided as to the extent of the Iranian people's opposition to the shah. In August 1978 the CIA reported that Iran was "not in a revolutionary or even a prerevolutionary situation." Carter was aware of the shah's tyranny, but, mindful of the anti-American sentiment of the ruler's opposition, Carter was fearful that the

> *It was becoming increasingly evident that the Shah was no longer functioning as a strong leader, but was growing despondent and unsure of himself.*
> —JIMMY CARTER

Soviet Union would seek to take advantage of the destabilization that was certain to occur if the shah were to be ousted. Carter's advisers counseled him against making an initiative to the dissidents. In late October 1978, William Sullivan, the American ambassador to Iran, cabled Washington with the assessment that "the shah is the unique element which can, on the one hand, restrain the military, and on the other hand, lead a controlled transition. . . . I would strongly oppose any overture to Khomeini." Relying on this advice, Carter agreed that U.S. strategic interests would best be served by continuing to prop up the shah while pressing him to institute liberalizing reforms.

Despite the optimism of Sullivan and the CIA, the shah's regime was doomed. He fled Iran on January 16, 1979. Khomeini arrived soon afterward and established himself as the nation's supreme political authority. The shah's exile took him from Egypt to Morocco to the Bahamas to Panama. His preferred

Republican presidential nominee Ronald Reagan (left) and his campaign manager, William Casey, are in good spirits at a campaign-strategy meeting in June 1980. There was no such merriment in the Democratic camp; public opinion of President Carter was reaching a new low.

destination was the United States, but Carter feared anti-American reprisals by the Iranians and initially refused to grant him sanctuary. In October 1979, Carter was told that the shah was suffering from cancer. Such influential Americans as Henry Kissinger and David Rockefeller, chairman of Chase Manhattan Bank and the head of the Trilateral Commission, beseeched Carter to let the shah enter the country for medical treatment unavailable to him in Mexico, where he was then taking refuge. Against his better judgment and despite warnings from the U.S. embassy in Teheran, Carter approved the shah's entry on October 20. Approximately two weeks later his worst fears were realized when Iranian militants overran the American embassy in Teheran.

Carter spent his last year in office trying to bring the hostages safely home. For many Americans, Carter's inability to obtain a swift resolution to the crisis was proof of his ineffectuality as president.

I believe the taint of the Shah being in our country is not good for either us or him.
—JIMMY CARTER

Waving to crowds at the Rhein-Main Air Base in West Germany, on January 21, 1981, Jimmy Carter awaits the return of the American hostages. As if to spite Carter, the Iranians waited until he had completed his final day in office before releasing the captives.

Iran had instituted an oil embargo against the United States following the shah's ouster, resulting in fuel shortages, higher prices, and long lines at gas stations. Carter had expended much time and effort on his energy program, but for the average voter the concrete benefits were hard to see. Carter had promoted himself as a prudent fiscal manager, but four years after his presidency began, inflation and unemployment continued to play havoc with the economy. Despite his failure with the shah, Carter's emphasis on human rights resulted in a lessening of oppression in nations such as Haiti and Nicaragua, but many Americans remembered only that he had given away "their" canal in Panama. The image of the president who had promised never to lie and had emphasized the need for moral values in government was further tarnished by financial scandals involving his close friend and adviser Bert Lance and his colorful younger brother, Billy. Reagan benefited from all these issues during the 1980 presidential campaign. Few questioned Carter's integrity, but many doubted that he was an effective leader. Many Americans might have agreed with Carter that the country was in a malaise, but that did not make them any fonder of the messenger who brought such tidings. Reagan won an overwhelming victory in November.

After his defeat, Carter and his family returned to Plains. Carter's Warehouse and the other family businesses had suffered financial reverses during his years in the White House, so Carter decided to sell the warehouse to pay off some debts. Much of Carter's time was spent organizing the records of his years in office for the Carter Presidential Center, which opened in Atlanta, Georgia, in October 1986 and is certain to prove an invaluable resource for historians studying the Carter years. Carter himself wrote five books during his first eight years out of office. *Keeping Faith*, his presidential memoirs,

Citizen Jimmy Carter and a fellow volunteer renovate a derelict building in New York City in 1984. Following his years in the Oval Office, Carter participated in a national effort to create affordable housing for people of low and middle incomes. He also published several books and began teaching at Emory University in Georgia.

Elder statesman Jimmy Carter flashes a characteristically benevolent grin at the 1988 Democratic National Convention in Atlanta, Georgia. Though the American public is perhaps more likely to remember Carter's failings than his achievements, the Carter years saw great heights as well as great lows.

was published in 1982. Carter is also the author of *The Blood of Abraham*, an examination of the historical roots of the ongoing strife in the Middle East; *Negotiation: The Alternative to Hostility*; *Everything to Gain*, an account, cowritten by Rosalynn, of the Carters' transition to life after the White House; and *An Outdoor Journal*, a reflection on fly-fishing and Carter's love of nature. Family also occupied much of the former president's time. The Carters have several grandchildren, and their youngest daughter, Amy, turned 20 in 1988. Carter relaxes by hunting, fishing, and woodworking, and he also donates several weeks each year to Habitat for Humanity, a missionary group that builds low-income housing.

It is difficult to predict how history will assess the Carter presidency. To some degree it will depend on how kind history is to his successor, Ronald Reagan, whose policies and personal style were diametrically opposed to Carter's. In 1984, Reagan was reelected — his opponent was Walter Mondale, Carter's vice-president — by an even greater margin than he won in 1980. Still, as the Reagan presidency came to an end in 1988, many Americans began to reassess the Carter years and to see the man himself in a new light.

Very few Americans would question Carter's sincerity, and most Americans admire Carter's dedication and determination. Unwilling to compromise his principles, Carter often took unpopular positions on extremely difficult issues, and he was always frank with the American people, even when the news was unpleasant to hear. He was an engaged U.S. president, struggling with the issues and personalities of his day with intelligence. A true diplomat, Carter proved that he was committed to peace through cooperation and negotiation and remained unwavering in his belief that no true peace can be gained by the use of brute force. Carter wrote in his memoirs that, like Thomas Jefferson, he took pride in the fact that not one American life was lost in a war during his presidency. Historically that is certainly a praiseworthy achievement.

> *I believe that history will speak better of Jimmy Carter than do his contemporary judges.*
> —BRUCE MAZLISH
> Carter biographer

_____Further Reading_____

Baker, James Thomas. *A Southern Baptist in the White House.* Philadelphia, PA: Westminster, 1977.

Califano, Joseph A., Jr. *Governing America.* New York: Simon & Schuster, 1982.

Carter, Jimmy. *The Blood of Abraham.* New York: Houghton Mifflin, 1985.

——. *Keeping Faith: Memoirs of a President.* New York: Bantam, 1982.

——. *Negotiation: The Alternatives to Hostility.* Macon, GA: Mercer University Press, 1984.

——. *Why Not the Best?* New York: Bantam, 1976.

Carter, Rosalynn. *First Lady from Plains.* New York: Fawcett, 1985.

Germond, Jack. *Blue Smoke and Mirrors: How Reagan Won & Why Carter Lost The Election of 1980.* New York: Viking, 1981.

Jordan, Hamilton. *Crisis: The True Story of an Unforgettable Year in the White House.* New York: Berkley, 1983.

——. *The Last Year of the Carter Presidency.* New York: Putnam, 1982.

Kucharsky, David. *The Man from Plains.* New York: Harper & Row, 1976.

Lasky, Victor. *Jimmy Carter: The Man & The Myth.* New York: Marek, 1979.

Mazlish, Bruce, and Edwin Diamond. *Jimmy Carter: An Interpretive Biography.* New York: Simon & Schuster, 1979.

Miller, William Lee. *Yankee from Georgia.* New York: Times Books, 1978.

Molenhoff, Clark. *The President Who Failed: Carter Out of Control.* New York: Macmillan, 1980.

Wooten, James. *Dasher: The Roots and The Rising of Jimmy Carter.* New York: Summit, 1978.

Chronology

Oct. 1, 1924	Born James Earl Carter, Jr., in Archery, Georgia
1942	Enters the U.S. Naval Academy at Annapolis
1946	Graduates from the U.S. Naval Academy; marries Rosalynn Smith
1951	Selected by Admiral Hyman Rickover to work on atomic submarine project
1952	James Earl Carter, Sr., father, dies; Carter returns to Plains to manage family business
1962	Carter elected to state senate
1970	Elected governor of Georgia
Dec. 1974	Announces presidential candidacy
July 1976	Wins the Democratic party nomination
Nov. 1976	Elected president
1978	Senate ratifies the Panama Canal treaties; energy bills pass both houses of Congress; normalization of diplomatic relations with China
Mar. 1979	Signing of the Camp David accords
Nov. 1979	U.S. citizens taken hostage at the U.S. embassy in Teheran
1980	Hostage rescue mission fails
Nov. 1980	Carter loses presidential election to Ronald Reagan
Jan. 1981	Hostages released; Reagan inaugurated
1982	*Keeping Faith*, Carter's presidential memoirs, is published
Oct. 1986	Carter Presidential Center opens in Atlanta, Georgia

Index

Ed Slavin is currently counsel to the Occupational Health Legal Rights Foundation (AFL-CIO) and was attorney-adviser to the chief judge of the U.S. Department of Labor Office of Administrative Law Judges in Washington, D.C. A graduate of the Georgetown University School of Foreign Service and Memphis State University Law School, he founded the *Appalachian Observer*, a Tennessee weekly newspaper focusing on major social and political issues.

Arthur M. Schlesinger, jr., taught history at Harvard for many years and is currently Albert Schweitzer Professor of the Humanities at City University of New York. He is the author of numerous highly praised works in American history and has twice been awarded the Pulitzer Prize. He served in the White House as special assistant to Presidents Kennedy and Johnson.

PICTURE CREDITS

AP/Wide World Photos: pp. 28, 34, 36, 43, 46, 88; The Jimmy Carter Library: pp. 24, 40; UPI/Bettmann Newsphotos: pp. 2, 12, 15, 16, 17, 18, 19, 20, 21, 23, 26, 31, 33, 38, 42, 44, 45, 48, 50, 52, 54, 55, 56, 57, 58, 59, 60, 62, 64, 66, 67, 68, 69, 70, 71, 72, 74, 76, 79, 80, 83, 84, 86, 90–91, 93, 96–97, 98, 100, 102–3, 104, 105, 106